GARLAND STUDIES ON

THE ELDERLY
IN AMERICA

edited by
STUART BRUCHEY
ALLAN NEVINS PROFESSOR EMERITUS
COLUMBIA UNIVERSITY

A GARLAND SERIES

FAMILY CRIMES AGAINST THE ELDERLY

ELDER ABUSE AND THE CRIMINAL JUSTICE SYSTEM

_____

PATRICIA J. BROWNELL

GARLAND PUBLISHING, INC.
A MEMBER OF THE TAYLOR & FRANCIS GROUP
NEW YORK & LONDON / 1998

Library of Congress Cataloging-in-Publication Data

Brownell, Patricia J., 1943–
    Family crimes against the elderly : elder abuse and the
criminal justice system / Patricia J. Brownell.
        p.   cm. — (Garland studies on the elderly in America)
    Includes bibliographical references and index.
    ISBN 0-8153-3209-2 (alk. paper)
    1. Abused aged—United States. 2. Aged—Abuse of—United
States. 3. Family violence—United States. 4. Social work with the
aged—United States. 5. Abused aged—Services for—United States.
6. Criminal justice, Administration of—United States.   I. Title.
II. Series.
HV6626.3.B73
364.1—dc21
                                                                98-39287

Printed on acid-free, 250-year-life paper
Manufactured in the United States of America

UNITED NATIONS PRINCIPLES FOR OLDER PERSONS

Older persons should be able to live in dignity and security and to be free of exploitation and physical and mental abuse. (United Nations General Assembly, 1991)

Contents

List of Tables

Foreword

Family Crimes Against the Elderly: A Study of Elder Abuse and the New York Police Department represents an important contribution to the available knowledge on elder abuse as a criminal justice issue. While most studies of elder abuse to date have examined this social problem from a health, mental health or social service perspective, few have focused on it from the perspective of law enforcement.

The effectiveness of the criminal justice system as an intervention strategy for elder abuse was one of the key research questions posed by a select group of experts on aging at an advisory meeting sponsored by the National Center on Elder Abuse and Neglect in 1990. Studying this poses formidable challenges, however. This is due to the confidential nature of police reports and the possible harm that follow-up by researchers may cause to elder abuse victims who report crimes committed against them by family members and significant others.

This ground breaking volume lays the foundation for both a criminal justice and social work knowledge base on elder abuse. The original and pioneering study draws on police reports of elder abuse in a highly populated, racially and ethnically diverse city. The inclusion of racial and ethnic diversity in the study reflects an emergent area of interest in the field: elder abuse in minority populations.

A second variable of interest examined in Dr. Brownell's study is that of stated willingness by the elderly victims in the sample to prosecute their offspring abusers. A high proportion of victims not only self-reported the abuse to the police, but also stated they were willing to prosecute their abusers at the time the complaint was filed. This challenges a prevailing stereotype of unempowered elder abuse victims who are unwilling to engage law enforcement as a strategy to end abuse by family members.

Finally, Dr. Brownell's study sets a precedent for a continued dialogue between the disciplines of social work and criminal justice by developing an interdisciplinary framework for examining elder abuse. Not only does it establish a common language to facilitate discussion between the two disciplines, but it suggests possibilities for collaboration that have potential for generating effective interventions into the serious social problem of family abuse and maltreatment of the elderly.

Dr. Brownell has more than 30 years of experience as a social worker, case manager, policy analyst, and administrator for the New York City Human Resources Administration (HRA); as a criminal justice/social work researcher, and as a university professor. She also has numerous publications to her credit. During the past decade, Dr. Brownell's research has focused on police interventions, elder abuse, female offenders, domestic violence and child abuse prevention, and correctional social work. I first became acquainted with Dr. Patricia Brownell's important research four years ago when I was putting together two author teams of leading experts in the fields of family violence and correctional social work. Dr. Brownell contributed two outstanding chapters as follows:

Patricia Brownell (1996), "Social work and criminal justice responses to elder abuse in New York City", in A. R. Roberts, *Helping Battered Women: New Perspectives and Remedies.* New York, N. Y.: Oxford University Press, pp. 44-66. This book includes original specially written chapters on family violence throughout the lifespan. Dr. Brownell was invited to write the elder abuse chapter because she is the only prolific scholar in the United States with expertise on both criminal justice and social work responses to elder abuse.

Patricia Brownell (1997), "Female offenders in the criminal justice system: policy and program development." in A. R. Roberts, second edition, *Social Work in Juvenile and Criminal Justice Settings.* Springfield, IL.: Charles C. Thomas, pp. 325-349.

I congratulate Dr. Brownell on this excellent and comprehensive contribution to the professional research literature. All criminal justice and social work researchers should purchase this important book for their university, agency, and/or personal libraries. I highly recommend this book as a "must read" for all family violence and gerontology researchers.

Albert R. Roberts, Ph.D.
Professor of Social Work and Criminal Justice
Rutgers University School of Social Work
Piscataway, New Jersey

Acknowledgments

I wish to extend special thanks to my Dissertation Committee members, each of whom offered me exceptional support and expert consultation. These included Dr. Michael Phillips, my Dissertation Chair, Professor Marjorie Cantor and Dr. Joseph Ryan.

Staff of the Office of Management, Analysis, and Planning (OMAP), especially Sergeant Daniel Parente and Police Officer Leslie Cardona-Matten, as well as members of the Legal Department, New York City Police Department, extended themselves to assist me in data gathering and information sharing, and played a very special role in the development of this dissertation project.

I am very grateful for the encouragement and support of my Supervisor at the Human Resources Administration (HRA), Mary Nakashian, Executive Deputy Commissioner for the Family Support Administration (FSA), as well as HRA Commissioner/Administrator Barbara J. Sabol and all my colleagues in the FSA Executive Office. HRA Associate General Counsel Richard O'Halleron provided expert assistance to this project and I extend special thanks to him as well.

To Mary and Dr. Robert Golden, I am greatly indebted for their invaluable roles as editorial and statistical consultants, respectively. Anne Goldstein did an excellent job in preparing the dissertation for final submission.

Family Crimes
against the Elderly

CHAPTER I
Problem Statement

INTRODUCTION

Elder abuse is an area of increasing concern for gerontologists and others in the helping professions. The United States House of Representatives Select Committee on Aging issued a report in 1990, *Elder Abuse: A Decade of Shame and Inaction*, which included the finding that one out of every 20 older Americans, or more than 1.5 million people, may be victims of elder abuse. The report also stated that elder abuse is far less likely to be reported than child abuse: While one out of every three child abuse cases is reported, only one out of eight cases of elder abuse cases is reported.

There is cause for concern for a number of reasons. First and primary is concern about the pain, risk, and danger to which abused elders are exposed. In addition, demographic studies point to the increasing number of aged people in our society, a phenomenon known as the graying of America (Gilford, 1988). Even if the proportion of abused elders in the population (currently estimated at between 3%-12% of the elderly) remained constant, the sheer numbers can be expected to increase.

Because elder abuse is considered to be a severely underreported as a form of domestic violence, identifying means of case finding becomes important. Mandatory reporting of elder abuse has been legislated in a number of states; however, research into its effectiveness as a means of detecting elder abuse has shown it to be limited

(Fredrikson, 1989). Some researchers have suggested that it is ageist and a violation of the right to self-determination of many older adults (Crystal, 1987; Faulkner, 1982). In addition, Johnson (1986) has questioned whether it should not be the decision of the victim—as opposed to the professional onlooker—as to what constitutes abuse.

Concerns such as these are reflected in the growing professional interest in the diversity of older people and the meanings they assign to events in their world. Without some means of identifying abuse and mistreatment of the elderly, however, possibilities for intervention are limited.

Adult protective service (APS) programs operate in every state to serve mentally and physically impaired adults, including older victims of domestic violence. These programs provide an important means of detection and intervention of situations involving abuse of older adults by relatives and significant others. APS programs generally limit their services to the frail and judgement impaired, however, not to the competent adult. As defined in the New York State (NYS) Social Services law, protective services even of an involuntary nature may be provided to judgement-impaired adults (18 years of age and older) who are unable to protect themselves from abuse and exploitation by others. This may include elders suffering from dementia (such as Alzheimer's Disease) whose needs are overwhelming caregivers. In these latter cases, case management and social services are usually considered the interventions of choice.

Another important but overlooked source of case finding for elder abuse is the criminal justice system—most notably, local police departments. This provides a means of addressing abuse and exploitation against older adults that reflect categories of actions defined by the penal code as constituting criminal acts.

ELDER ABUSE AND THE CRIMINAL JUSTICE SYSTEM

Research on the role of the criminal justice system as an intervention strategy in elder abuse is needed, but is considered inadequate to date (NARCEA, 1991). This reflects difficulty with access to information even at the local law enforcement level. Several reasons include:

1. Police departments do not generally maintain domestic violence information in a form that is accessible to researchers.
2. Confidentiality mandates keep much of the recorded information on complaint reports unavailable to researchers, or to service providers such as APS, home care vendors, and not-for-profit social service workers.
3. Special computer programs are generally required to identify crimes against specific age groups—like the elderly—by relationship to perpetrator and type of crime.
4. Offenses as defined by the Uniform Crime Reports are not always comparable to accepted definitions of elder abuse in the literature.

As a result, much information captured through police complaint reports on elder abuse is incomplete (e.g., information is missing on the forms) or unavailable to researchers, policy makers, and practitioners (Saltzman et al., 1990).

There have been few significant studies to date either on the use of complaint reports to assess patterns of family violence or to investigate the police response to domestic elder abuse. Two notable exceptions are, on the former, "Magnitude and Patterns of Family and Intimate Behavior in Atlanta, Georgia, 1984" (Saltzman et al., 1990), and—on the latter—*A Time for Dignity: Police and Domestic Abuse of the Elderly* (Plotkin, 1988). The Saltzman study, however, did not examine elder abuse as a form of domestic violence, and the study by Plotkin (a collaborative effort between the Police Executive Research Forum and the American Association of Retired Persons) is currently out of print. This latter study also focused more on procedures implemented in local law enforcement agencies throughout the United States identifying and responding to elder abuse than on examining actual case situations.

In spite of the paucity of research utilizing police data to investigate elder abuse, these data are collected by all police departments throughout the country (Plotkin, 1988). The Plotkin study, in fact, identified the New York City Police Department (NYPD) as exemplary in its efforts on behalf of victims of domestic violence, including elderly victims of mistreatment. In 1989, for example, 4,000 incidents of domestic violence were reported to the NYPD (New York City Elder Abuse Coalition, 1990). Although staff shortages have limited the capacity of the NYPD to retrieve information on elder abuse as captured on complaint reports, it is possible to make such identifications through special computer programming.

POLICE COMPLAINT REPORTS AS SOURCE OF INFORMATION AND CASE FINDING

Information captured on the complaint report (Appendix C) can provide important descriptive information on demographic and structural aspects of elder abuse. In addition, because the abuse incident is reported either by or on behalf of elderly victims at the time of the abusive incident, it is likely to represent the victim's perception of having suffered mistreatment. Finally, because the complaint report also includes a brief narrative description of the abusive event—either as reported by the victim or witness, it provides a more vivid picture of the nature of the event than statistical data or crime codes alone.

These reports provide useful information on elder abuse from the criminal justice perspective; they are also useful in beginning to build a bridge between the fields of criminology and of gerontology, sociology, and social work. However, knowing descriptive information on elder abuse victims who come into contact with the criminal justice system is not sufficient to ensure that these victims receive needed protection from the abuser (perpetrator), or that the abuser is either sanctioned or provided with needed corrective services. In order for elder abuse to be addressed through the criminal justice system, the victims must be willing in most cases to prosecute the abuser. For the purposes of this study, prosecution can take the form of cooperating with the police and/or District Attorney or seeking an order of protection through either criminal or family courts.

In New York City, at the time of the completion of the crime report by the police (when responding to a complaint by or on behalf of the victim), the victim is asked whether he or she would be willing to prosecute the perpetrator. The response is recorded on the complaint report. While the victim may change his or her mind subsequently as to whether to follow through with prosecution, answering in the affirmative at the time of the initial contact will normally initiate a follow-up response from a detective at the local precinct. At this time, encouragement and support for the victim to follow through with prosecution could allow for intervention utilizing the criminal justice system, a desirable outcome in that it could result in possible deterrent to future abuse, or as a vehicle for involving social service providers.

DOMESTIC VIOLENCE VICTIMS AND WILLINGNESS TO PROSECUTE

The use of prosecution in domestic violence situations is a controversial one (Mancuso, 1989). The goal of the Family Court system in New York, for example, is to help family members work out problems outside the criminal justice system. Subsequently, as victims' rights advocates began to challenge the use of civil court to adjudicate crimes committed by family members against spouses, the option of using criminal court for this purpose was legislated.

Borrowing from the spouse abuse literature, it is argued that a victim's decision to prosecute his or her abuser is a desirable outcome if it can serve to protect the elderly victim against further abuse. This can signal to an abuser that the victim is refusing to continue an abusive relationship. It can also result—assuming appropriate follow-through on the part of the victim—in at a minimum an order of protection being issued, permitting immediate arrest by police if the abuser violates its conditions. This may include an arrest with alternatives to incarceration such as requiring the abuser to enter substance abuse or mental health treatment. An order of protection forbids the abuser to contact the victim for a defined period of time; a violation of this results in mandatory arrest of the offender.

Police reports on elder abuse could also provide an important and often overlooked source of case finding, if the victim states willingness to prosecute and therefore receives a follow-up contact by the local precinct. In a state like New York, which is one of eight states with no mandatory reporting system, police reports could provide valuable information on incidence and prevalence of abuse in communities.

Stating willingness to prosecute an abuser who is a family member, such as an offspring (child), could increase an elder abuse victim's sense of empowerment and the likelihood of making a decision to establish limits for an abusive offspring. Finally, it could lead to intervention by social workers collaborating with police officers to target those elder abuse victims who come to the attention of the police for follow-up services.

Services offered through such a collaboration could include supporting a victim's decision to prosecute and/or to support the victim through the prosecution process. For victims who refuse to state willingness to prosecute their abuser, the appropriateness of a referral to Adult Protective Services could be evaluated. Other service interventions could also include counseling and case management, linking the victim with the aging service network for assistance with securing broken locks and doors, providing meals on wheels, friendly visiting or telephone reassurance services, as well as respite and other services as needed. Evaluation of service needs of the abuser should not be overlooked, particularly if the abuser appears to be an overwhelmed caregiver (of an Alzheimer's patient, for example) or a developmentally disabled or mentally or physically impaired adult. To enhance this social work role, it would be useful to recognize a profile presented by victims who would most likely state willingness to prosecute as well as those who would not, in order to more effectively target efforts on their behalf.

PURPOSE OF STUDY

The purpose of this study is four-fold:

1. To develop a descriptive profile of elder abuse as reported to NYPD. Victims residing in Manhattan have been selected as the study sample. Based on the proportion of its elderly residents compared with the rest of the population in New York City and the diversity of its ethnic composition, this borough provides a representative framework within which to examine the problem of elder abuse (New York City Department for the Aging [DFTA], 1993).

2. To expand the knowledge base of types of criminal offenses committed against older people by their off-spring, and identify frameworks for translating criminal justice terminology into categories of elder abuse already established by gerontologists, sociologists and protective service statutes.

3. To test the hypothesis that it is possible to predict—based on information from police complaint police reports—which elderly victims of domestic mistreatment who come to the attention of local law enforcement agencies will be willing to prosecute their abusers.

4. To utilize the findings of the study to make recommendations to the law enforcement and social service communities regarding collaborative efforts that may be jointly undertaken to increase the safety and quality of life of older community residents in Manhattan.

CHAPTER II

Literature Review

DOMESTIC VIOLENCE

In 1978, Suzanne Steinmetz introduced the concept of elder abuse during a congressional hearing on domestic violence. Since then, considerable interest has been focused on this issue by representatives of many different disciplines (Anetzburger, 1987). This includes primarily professionals in gerontology, sociology, medicine, and nursing. The disciplines of social work and criminology have been less involved in an examination of this phenomenon.

In relation to social work, this is in part due to the fact that concerns about services to the elderly have traditionally taken a backseat to concerns about children and families. Fordham University Graduate School of Social Work, for example, has one of the few doctoral-level curricula devoted to social welfare concerns of the aged. This is in spite of the fact that our society is increasingly an aging one, with almost one in five projected to be over the age of 65 by the year 2025 (Table 1).

Within the discipline of criminology, victimology is a fairly new subspecialty. Until the 1970s, more attention was paid to the criminal than the victim. The civil rights movement is generally credited with raising the level of concern regarding those members of society who have been prevented from experiencing social justice (Fattah & Sacco, 1989). During the 1960s, as issues of social justice were coming to the fore, child abuse was identified as a social issue of concern. During the

1970s, spouse abuse was raised as an issue by feminists, and the 1980s have been identified as "the decade of elder abuse" (Wolf, 1988).

Table 1: Elderly Population as Percentage of Total Population: Selected Years 1980-2025

	1980	1990	2000[a]	2025[a]
Population 65 years and older (in thousands)	26,125	31,995	35,682	61,480
Population age 65 and older as a percentage of total population	11.1	12.3	12.6	18.8

Source: 1991 Annual Report of the Board of Trustees of the Federal Old-Age and Survivors Insurance and Disability Insurance Trust funds, and unpublished estimates of the Actuary, Social Security Administration (U.S. House of Representatives, 1993).

Domestic violence in general, which includes child, spouse, and elder abuse, is a complex issue for both criminology and social work in that it is not a stranger crime. Rather, the perpetrator and victim are both intimately known to each other, often in ways that include not only emotional involvement, but financial and social support as well. More importantly, with a stranger criminal offense, the victim is not likely to encounter the offender again. However, in family offense cases the victims are often repeatedly, on a daily basis, exposed to their abusers.

These close ties between victim and perpetrator often confound the more traditional ways each discipline has evolved for ensuring safety and protection of the victim, redress for the crime, and punishment of the perpetrator. In fact, because of the emotional ties between victim and perpetrator, it is believed that often the victim refuses to implicate the perpetrator, thus preventing the involvement of the criminal justice system (U.S. House of Representatives, 1990).

In the case of child abuse, clear-cut laws have been passed ensuring that the unwillingness or inability of the child-victim to implicate the perpetrator does not act as a barrier to involvement of the perpetrator in the criminal justice system. This is through invocation of the right of *parens patriae*: Because the child is a legal minor, the state has the right to intercede on his or her behalf acting as surrogate guardian (Gelles, 1987).

For spouse abuse, the situation is complicated by the fact that the victim is a legal adult with the right to self-determination. In these situations, social work interventions stress empowerment and in New York State, for example, laws generally give victims the right to seek redress or protection from perpetrators in either family or criminal courts. Some studies have demonstrated that prosecution and imprisonment of the perpetrator of spouse abuse have a deterrent effect on future abuse, but nonetheless require the active participation of the victim in the prosecution process (Goleman, 1991; Sherman & Cohn, 1990).

Similarly in the case of elder abuse victims who are not incapacitated, intervention strategies that stress empowerment have been suggested as the most effective and appropriate (Breckman & Adelman, 1988). Advocates for the elderly, practitioners and researchers who promote this perspective underline the point that elderly are adults, not children, and this should be respected unless it appears their decisional capacity is impaired to the extent that they are unable to protect themselves against abuse or exploitation by others (Crystal, 1987; Faulkner, 1982).

Because advanced age can be correlated with physical and mental frailty, some older adults may not be capable of advocating on their own behalf or protecting themselves from exploitation or mistreatment, even with expert counseling and support. In addition, their care needs may exceed the capacity of even well-meaning caregivers to respond adequately and appropriately. Another intervention strategy for addressing elder abuse is that of relieving stress on caregivers. Many early studies on elder abuse (Lau & Kosberg, 1979; Steinmetz, 1981) focused on cases that came to the attention of family agencies. Findings suggested that elder abuse stemmed from family breakdown under pressures of caring for an impaired older relative.

DEFINITION OF ELDER ABUSE

Elder abuse is defined here as physical, psychological, or financial abuse by a family member who is a son, daughter, son- or daughter-in-law, step-son or daughter, niece or nephew, or grandchild. Physical abuse can include hitting, pushing, or use of a weapon where physical contact occurred. Psychological abuse can include threatening, intimidating, harassing, insulting, or other behavior that causes concern on the part of the victim, but does not involve physical contact. Financial abuse is defined as exploiting an older person financially, such as taking or attempting to take his or her assets, income, or property through intimidation or without consent.

CLASSIFICATION SCHEMA FOR TYPES OF ABUSE

These three categories of elder abuse are commonly used in New York City and reflect a categorical schema that was originally developed by Wolf and Pillemer (1984). A fourth category, neglect (active and passive), is not utilized in the present study as it does not easily lend itself to translation into the criminal offenses as defined by the NYS Penal Code. Neglect includes the unintentional or deliberate withholding of medication, food, clothing, or other goods and services associated with caregiving. Unless the withholder is a formal or legally designated caregiver, such as a home attendant or a court appointed guardian, for example, or unless care is being withheld because funds belonging to the elder are being misappropriated by the informal caregiver (family member or significant other), such actions are not codified as offenses to be addressed by the NYS criminal justice system. As noted, New York State is one of eight states that do not have mandatory reporting systems for elder abuse.

Other classifications have been developed, most notably by researcher Tanya Johnson (1991). Her categories of types of abuse include physical, psychological, sociological, and legal. While her physical and psychological categories of abuse closely conform to those in use in New York City, her sociological category includes such factors as isolation, role confusion, and misuse of living arrangements, including household disorganization, lack of privacy, unfit environment, and abandonment.

These categories may be useful for adult protective service workers investigating a neglect complaint; however, they have limited application for law enforcement agents investigating a complaint regarding a criminal offense against an older person by an offspring. The legal category is—in the view of this researcher—misleading, since it focuses on financial abuse and ignores the fact that other forms of abuse and mistreatment of older persons—rape or assault, for example—have legal implications as well.

As a result of comparing Johnson's and other elder abuse classification schemes with that developed by Pillemer and Wolf and supported by the New York City Elder Abuse Coalition (a coalition of public and private agencies serving the elderly), the Pillemer and Wolf model has been selected as the definitional frame for abuse for the purposes of this study. It is most commonly used in New York City, from which the elder abuse sample has been drawn, as well as in New York State. It also appears to most closely conform with categories of criminal offenses (as defined in the New York State Penal Code) against the elderly by family members.

CASE FINDING

A key concern of domestic violence advocates and researchers is that family abuse is a hidden problem. Incidence and prevalence of abuse is difficult to ascertain as family members attempt to conceal the abuse out of shame and fear (Pillemer & Suitor, 1988; Steinmetz, 1978). In states where reporting is not mandatory, the problem of identifying abuse is even more difficult. As a result, instances of abuse may not come to public attention and available protective interventions may not come into play.

In the context of social services and case management for the elderly, one key component is protective services. At minimum, reporting abuse to the police means bringing it to the attention of law enforcement that, when appropriate, can seek to separate the abuser from the victim and/or focus the victim's family on the need for social service assistance. If victims or concerned family members or observers take no action in response to the abuse, it will not come to the attention of authorities or service professionals who can assist victims to increase their safety and security.

Elder abuse is also complicated, as in the case of spouse abuse, by the legal status of the victim as an adult considered to be responsible for self-determination unless found incompetent by a court of law. However, in addition, it is also complicated by the fact that advanced age can add a differential factor that is not always predictable in terms of its impact on the victim's ability to act independently and with competent judgment regarding the implication of the perpetrator in the abusive act (Pillemer & Finkelhor, 1989).

Some studies have suggested that elderly victims of abuse by family members are especially reluctant to report the abuse to helping professionals, much less to authorities within the criminal justice system. Various reasons have been posited for this, including fear of retribution, loyalty to abuser (perpetrator), concern about losing support and being moved to a nursing home, and other factors (Fulmer & O'Malley, 1987).

All 50 states have protective services laws for adults aged 18 and above. In response to pressures from advocates for the aged, a number of state legislatures have also passed mandatory reporting laws. In the case of mandatory reporting, certain categories of professionals—as defined in the statutes—are required by law to report suspected or actual cases of elder abuse to either social service (generally public or under contract to a public social services or aging agency) or law enforcement agencies—usually through contacting a state central registry, similar to that used for reporting child abuse.

For states such as New York, which do not have a mandatory reporting system for elder abuse, professionals and other concerned parties (including the victim) can make a report to the local Adult Protective Services (APS) office (Plotkin, 1988). However, unless either the identified victims or perpetrators are impaired to the extent of being a danger to themselves or others, or being unable to protect themselves, APS workers are often unable to provide assistance.

Both mandatory reporting and the availability of adult protective service programs as social policy responses to elder abuse reflect the perspective that elder abuse or mistreatment occurs because the older person is unable to protect or advocate for him or herself. An alternative perspective, as reflected in recent studies—most notably by Pillemer and Finkelhor (1988), is that older people who are victims of domestic violence are often the caretaker relatives of dependent adult children. This perspective suggests that in fact older people can be empowered to, and in fact often do, advocate on their own behalf by bringing an abuse situation to the attention of social service agencies or law enforcement authorities. This lends support for the notion that the criminal justice system is another (often overlooked) resource for the detection, assessment, and intervention of elder abuse cases.

PROFILES OF ELDER ABUSE

A number of theories on the etiology of elder abuse have been proposed in the literature. Two of the most prominent are those proposed by Karl Pillemer, a sociologist, and Suzanne Steinmetz, a psychologist and domestic violence expert. Steinmetz, whose initial investigations into domestic violence included studies on child and spouse abuse, has suggested that elder abuse may be primarily associated with caretaker stress (Steinmetz, 1981). This conforms with the findings of many of the early studies on elder abuse: that the elder most at risk of abuse is a woman over the age of 75 with severe impairments and care needs, who is being cared for by a close relative, often a middle-aged daughter or daughter-in-law with other family responsibilities (Block & Sinnott, 1979). In Steinmetz' model, it is the caretaker daughter who is the family member most likely to abuse the elderly parent under her care, in response to the overwhelming stress of addressing the elder's care needs.

Pillemer, on the other hand, the author of a groundbreaking study of elders in Boston considered to be one of the most methodologically sound of all the studies on elder abuse to date (Wolf, 1992), has suggested an alternative explanation of elder abuse based on the findings of his study (Pillemer & Finkelhor, 1988). In his model, the elder most at risk of abuse is the unimpaired young-old (60 to 74 year old) caregiver relative (most likely parent) of an impaired dependent adult child (most likely son). An example is that of a 66-year-old man who lives with his 32 year old son who is unemployed and an alcoholic. The father provides shelter, food, and tries to assist his son with money management; the son in turn is verbally abusive and on occasion cashes his father's social security check without his permission to buy alcohol.

One reason suggested for this model of elder abuse is that to serve as a caretaker relative of an adult child, the parent must be reasonably unimpaired and capable of providing the necessary level of support (at least initially). However, in Pillemer's model, as discussed below, the parent is thought to be at risk of abuse because the abuser perceives the relationship as socially unacceptable: The abuse occurs as an effort on the part of the dependent adult child to obtain a position of power in relation to the caretaker parent.

The theoretical underpinnings of both models described above are variations of sociological theories of aging (Passuth & Bengston, 1988). Pillemer suggests that social exchange theory, which posits that relationships between people are based on the balance of power between them, explains the etiology of elder abuse in these cases. In most relationships between young and old, the elderly are seen as lacking power in relation to the young because they have fewer resources and lower status within society. In the case of older people providing care to impaired adult children, however, Pillemer suggests that the normative power relation is reversed and the younger adult is abusive as a strategy to regain power or redress the perceived power imbalance (Wolf, 1990).

Steinmetz, on the other hand, proposes an alternative explanation—social breakdown theory, an application of symbolic interactionism—to conform to her model of elder abuse. She suggests that social breakdown theory provides a useful explanation for the phenomenon of abuse in situations where the caregiver is overwhelmed with the care needs of the elderly relative and reacts with abuse out of frustration. One of the reasons for this is that the older person has defined his or (usually in this model) her position as one of helplessness and weakness, and the caregiver has defined his or (usually) her position as one of needing to provide all the elder's care needs as part of the role of caregiver. This places stress on both caregiver and care receiver, and their interaction can lead to abuse (Steinmetz, 1988).

An example is that of an 86-year-old woman who lives with her 50-year-old daughter. The daughter is employed and is also a single mother of two teen-aged sons. Because the daughter is pressed for time, she chooses her mother's meals and clothing and restricts her activities so she does not fall and injure herself—as she had the previous year. The mother is resentful, bored, and increasingly passive, placing more pressure on the daughter to make decisions and perform tasks on her behalf. This in turn causes the daughter to feel more stressed and overwhelmed, resulting in escalating household tension, arguments (which may include pushing and slapping), and threats of nursing home placement. While Steinmetz focuses on the elderly, this phenomenon has also been cited as related to abuse of children and the handicapped.

An important implication of using social exchange and social breakdown theories as explanatory underpinnings of elder abuse is in the intervention strategies that follow from them. The use of social exchange theory suggests that the balance of power must be equalized for the abusive situation to be rectified. By assisting the abuser to address his or her dependency on the elderly victim, the abuser's need to assert control over the victim in a destructive way may be ameliorated. Job training, substance abuse and mental health treatment, adult day treatment, and socialization skills training are possible intervention strategies targeting the abuser. Alternatively, sanctions imposed on the abuser may increase the costs in continuing the abusive behavior and serve to discourage future abuse. The victim may be assisted to redefine his or her relationship with the abuser from being a protector (and possible enabler) to playing a role in his or her rehabilitation (Wolf, 1990).

Using social breakdown theory as an explanation of elder abuse, an intervention strategy that addresses learned helplessness on the part of the victim and teaches the abuser/caregiver to set limits, achieve greater competency in performing caregiving tasks, and utilize both informal and formal supports more effectively would be indicated.

Here, both victim and abuser are engaged in developing a greater sense of competency within their assessed capacity so that the victim does not feel unstimulated and dominated and the caregiver unduly overwhelmed and frustrated.

DOMESTIC VIOLENCE AND THE CRIMINAL JUSTICE SYSTEM

In 1977, a lawsuit known as Bruno v. Codd, brought by Marjory Fields, then of the Brooklyn Legal Services Corp. B, Family Law Unit, against the New York City Police Department and the family court's probation department, resulted in a signed consent degree that established a policy of affirmative arrest for domestic violence cases. This means that an arrest in a misdemeanor case must be made if the domestic violence victim requests it. In addition, the policy has a mandatory component, in that for a felony charge (punishable by a minimum of one year in prison), an arrest must be made regardless of whether or not the victim requests it. In practical terms, however, a conviction is difficult if the victim refuses to press charges.

Some studies on spouse abuse have suggested that prosecution of abusers in domestic violence situations may be seen not only as a positive step toward acknowledgment of abuse and self-protection, but may also have a deterrent effect on future abuse incidents as well (Mancuso, 1989). This concept is supported by feminist groups advocating for social justice for battered women, and has been challenged by advocates such as Gelles (1987) who advocate for the family crisis intervention approach. This approach stresses family mediation over prosecution. However, although there are several studies on the use of the criminal justice system as an intervention strategy in spouse abuse, the literature does not reflect similar studies undertaken with regard to elder abuse.

Several factors are cited in the literature as impeding investigation of elder abuse. One is that it is a fairly new concept that has yet to receive the same level of attention from social scientists as spouse or child abuse. Another is the perceived reluctance of elder abuse victims to step forward and identify themselves. According to a number of researchers, elder abuse is a vastly underreported phenomenon. Third is the ambiguity in definitions of elder abuse. One of the primary barriers in the systematic study of elder mistreatment is the controversy over the definition of what constitutes elder abuse. For example, Hudson (1989) and Johnson (1986, 1991) point out that what may seem to be abuse by a professional researcher or practitioner may in fact appear culturally normative to the elder person.

INTERDISCIPLINARY NATURE OF INQUIRY INTO ELDER ABUSE AS A CRIMINAL JUSTICE ISSUE

There is another overlooked reason for the lack of studies on the use of the criminal justice system as an intervention strategy in elder abuse (NARCEA, 1991). The interdisciplinary nature of an inquiry necessary to begin addressing this issue may in fact serve as another barrier. Because criminal justice and social work have traditionally maintained separate and rarely overlapping spheres, particularly in the realm of gerontology, it is not surprising that few cooperative studies have been undertaken.

This is unfortunate for several reasons. First, studies on crime and older adults have demonstrated that the elderly, perhaps more than any other age group, tend to trust and look toward the police for protection. On the other side, studies have also shown that the police tend to respond to complaints and concerns of the elderly positively and supportively (Yin, 1985). While the initial inquiries into elder abuse have come from the medical, social service, and social science fields, it would appear that the police could be useful allies in the detection and assessment of elder abuse, as well as intervention.

An important collaborative study between the American Association of Retired Persons (AARP) and the Police Executive Research Forum (PERF) is an example of one effort to examine the possibilities of utilizing law enforcement to address elder abuse (Plotkin, 1988). The study utilized surveys of police practitioners and other data gathering methods to:

> determine how the police perceive the scope and severity of elder abuse and neglect; determine the level of police awareness of legal mandates and related issues; examine how law enforcement currently

responds to the problem, and formulate recommendations that would guide the police response. (Plotkin, 1988, p. 3)

While law enforcement agencies have been identified as ranking fourth on a list of service resources citizens and practitioners would contact when seeking relief from elder abuse, behind medical, mental health, and social service agencies and institutions (Wolf et al., 1984), the AARP/PERF study found that law enforcement practitioners did not see elder abuse as a significant criminal justice problem. One exception was that of financial abuse and exploitation, in relation to which survey respondents saw a role for law enforcement agencies. Neglect was identified as the responsibility of adult protective services agencies and psychological abuse and neglect of concern to community-based family service agencies (Plotkin, 1988).

Among the law enforcement agencies surveyed, the New York City Police Department was prominent among those that identified domestic violence as an important crime issue to be addressed by the police. According to the NYPD respondent to the AARP/PERF elder abuse survey: "Police can be detectors. Police are the only ones working 24 hours a day and should be trained on indicators of abuse" (Plotkin, 1988, p. 100).

While law enforcement agencies have the potential for providing a rich source of information on elder abuse, it is difficult to collect data on elder abuse as reported to law enforcement agencies. As noted in the AARP/PERF study, current data collection and storage methods are ill-suited to retrieving information on this problem. While Uniform Crime Reports (UCR) are regularly analyzed and compiled by the United States Department of Justice, there is no such crime category as elder abuse or domestic violence per se. Any of the 30 UCR crime codes reported may reflect elder abuse, but crime analyses must extract age and relationship data separately.

Even when local law enforcement agencies have made efforts to report crimes against the elderly, relationships between victim and perpetrator are not generally identified (Plotkin, 1988). In a 1989 survey of domestic violence crimes reported to the NYPD, data on relationships between victim and perpetrator were included, but crimes identified as reflective of domestic violence were not inclusive. For example, financial related crimes—considered to be a significant type of crime against the elderly perpetrated by family relatives, especially off-spring—were not included. Examples include larceny, robbery, and forgery.

Most forms of elder abuse that come to the attention of law enforcement agencies are no different than crimes committed against non-related individuals. However, these criminal acts are categorized differently by the criminal justice system than by researchers in other fields such as gerontology. Alternatively, categories of elder abuse identified by the gerontological, sociological, social work, and adult protective services communities are not always easily translatable into terminology utilized by law enforcement.

For example, psychological or emotional abuse as defined in the elder abuse literature may be classified as menacing—either a Misdemeanor A or a Felony E, depending on circumstances, by the NYS penal code. As another example, harassment as a reportable offense may be also viewed as reflecting the elder abuse category of psychological abuse (as defined, for example, by Pillemer and Wolf). However, United States Department of Justice Bureau of Justice Statistics counts as crimes all attempts as well as successfully completed crimes (U.S. Department of Justice, 1981). Menacing or harassment for the purpose of obtaining money from the victim—even if the attempt is not successful—could be categorized as a form of financial abuse. To assume all reported incidents of menacing or harassment are forms of psychological abuse may be misleading if the goal is to translate reported incidents of criminal offenses against elderly victims by relatives into accepted categories of elder abuse as a form of domestic violence.

For the purposes of this study, for example, harassment with the intent of obtaining money and property (although ultimately unsuccessful) was categorized as a form of financial abuse. Also, harassment where the abuser also pushed or shoved the victim—even if no physical injuries resulted—was categorized as physical abuse. While harassment implies efforts to annoy or disturb and suggests psychological abuse, assuming harassment (as defined on the complaint report by the responding police officer) as *only* reflecting psychological abuse may be underestimating the amount of physical or financial abuse occurring. Another example is robbery, which would appear to be a clear example of financial abuse, but by definition also involves physical force or use of a weapon and could represent a form of physical abuse as well.

While such refinements could be made while translating criminal offenses against elderly victims by relatives into accepted categories of elder abuse, this is difficult to achieve without access to comprehensive narrative descriptions of the actual incidents. Computerized data reports do not supply this level of detail and confidentiality mandates on the part of law enforcement agencies make this information almost impossible to obtain for researchers.

ELDER ABUSE DETECTION AND THE NEW YORK CITY CRIMINAL JUSTICE SYSTEM

Conventional wisdom and many studies have attested to the hidden nature of domestic violence (and hence the difficulties posed in studying it); however, the NYPD in 1989 alone recorded over 4,000 incidents of what was categorized as domestic violence reported in the five boroughs of the city (Ryan, personal communication, 1990). As a way of addressing the definitional problems of what constitutes domestic violence, the NYPD identified a number of criminal acts—ranging from harassment through felonious assault with weapon—that are associated with domestic violence. Identification of reported criminal actions that the NYPD associated with domestic violence are included as Appendix A. Additional criminal actions more likely to be associated with elder abuse by off-spring than with child or spouse abuse are included in Appendix B.

When alleged crimes are committed and victims contact the police (or the police are contacted on their behalf), a complaint report is completed on the scene by the police with the victim and filed with the precinct, after which selected data are entered onto a central computer file. As noted previously, some information is dropped as part of this process, including data on willingness to prosecute on the part of the victim, and the narrative overview of the incident that is recorded by the police responding to the complaint based on the victim's or witness's description. While the original (hard) copies of the complaint reports are maintained in a central file section for a period of time and contain the additional information not data entered on each complaint, they are difficult for researchers to obtain. This is related both to confidentiality issues and the logistical problems associated with identifying, locating, and retrieving them.

Because of these challenges, few studies have been done utilizing actual complaint reports. One notable study that did utilize hard copies of complaint reports was undertaken in 1984 by Saltzman et al. (1990) in Atlanta, Georgia. This study concentrated on domestic violence generally, with an emphasis on child and spouse abuse, not elder abuse. This is not surprising as elder abuse is a relatively new category of domestic violence for research purposes (Anetzburger, 1987).

In spite of the challenges in obtaining hard copies of complaint reports reflecting elder abuse-related crimes, these provide a useful source of data through which to further our understanding of elder abuse. In addition, as noted above, the abuse situations examined through these data can be categorized according to alleged violation of criminal laws and—because of the narrative descriptions included with each report—compared to definitions of elder abuse from the existing literature.

Finally, because complaint reports reflect self-reports of abuse—or reports corroborated by the victim at the time of the complaint report, they eliminate for case finding purposes the possibly biased subjective judgment of a professional onlooker (such as a social worker, researcher, or health worker). Such bias has been a frequent criticism of mandatory reporting of elder abuse as a case-finding strategy (Wolf & McCarthy, 1991).

SIGNIFICANT VARIABLES IN ELDER ABUSE AS IDENTIFIED IN THE LITERATURE

As noted above, in spite of the relative newness of elder abuse as a social issue, a number of studies have been undertaken that are exploratory and descriptive in nature (Hudson & Johnson, 1986). These have identified factors that appear to be significant in describing, as well as detecting and assessing, elder abuse. While a cataloging of physical and psychological signs of abuse is beyond the scope of this study, other variables identified as significant include the age of the victim and abuser, gender of victim and abuser, type of abuse, relationship between victim and abuser including familial status and living arrangements, relative dependence/independence of victim in relation to abuser, and willingness of the victim to take responsibility for addressing the abuse (Chen, Bell, Dolinsky, Doyle, & Dunn, 1981; Sengstock & Liang, 1982; Wolf et al., 1984).

A number of studies have focused on the gender of both victim and abuser. As noted, early studies identified the victim/abuser dyad as most likely to be that of mother and daughter (Steinmetz, 1981). Later studies identified prevalence of abuse by sons against both mothers and fathers (Pillemer & Finkelhor, 1988). Anetzburger (1987) undertook a qualitative study of abuse against mothers by sons. Most recently, Vinton (1988) examined the relationship between gender and elder abuse as part of a dissertation project. She found that abused elders identified through the Wisconsin voluntary elder abuse reporting system were disproportionately female and perpetrators of maltreatment were primarily male relatives of the victims (Vinton, 1988).

Findings on these variables have not been consistent. For example, early studies of elder abuse using agency reports identified elderly (75 years of age and older) white women as most at risk of being abused, with middle-aged (presumably caretaker) daughters being the most likely abusers (Johnson, 1986). Other studies, most notably that of Anetzburger (1987), explored abuse of older women by middle-aged sons who were often performing caregiving roles for which they appeared unsuited. Pillemer, on the other hand, identified young-old (aged 60 to 74 years of age) people to be most frequently victimized by family members, with men as likely to be victimized as women. Among offspring abusers, dependent adult sons were more likely to be abusers than daughters (Pillemer & Finkelhor, 1989).

Most studies identify self-abuse and neglect as the most prevalent form of abuse. These may be reflected in Adult Protective Services (APS) cases, but are not likely to be reflected in police complaint reports. One APS study undertaken by the New York State Department of Social Services), which did not examine self-abuse as a form of elder abuse, found financial abuse to be the most frequent type of domestic abuse among APS cases (Abelman, 1992).

Race/ethnicity and the demographics of communities (which can correlate to income status) in which reported elder abuse victims reside are two variables that have not been studied extensively to date. One study on elder abuse among African Americans (Vinton & Williams, 1992) suggests that financial abuse may be more prevalent than other forms of abuse, most notably physical.

A second study comparing elder abuse among African-Americans and White older adults in Milwaukee County found that Black victims were more likely to be female than White victims, they tended to be victims of more serious abuse than Whites, they were not more likely to experience financial or physical abuse than Whites, and those who were physically abused tended to be older than victims of other types of abuse. This study, which used data from Wisconsin's voluntary elder abuse reporting system, also found that in the abuse group African Americans were overrepresented proportional to their estimated percentage of the county population (Longres, 1992).

The United States Department of Justice (1984) reported that Blacks tend to report domestic violence to local law enforcement agencies proportionally more than other ethnic/racial groups in seeking protection and redress against mistreatment by family members. Income status has not been found to be a significant factor in domestic violence, although low-income victims may be more likely to utilize the law enforcement system if unable to afford more discrete (and costly) forms of redress.

Studies on elder abuse among the Hispanic or Asian populations in the United States are almost non-existent, and those on Native Americans have to date been confined to subjects living on reservations as opposed to urban areas (Brown, 1989). The paucity of data on these ethnic groups provides little basis for more than a descriptive analysis of data available through NYPD. While "Native American" is one of the five ethnic categories used on the police complaint report to identify victims and perpetrators, Native American elders represent a negligible percentage of Manhattan residents according to the 1990 census report (New York City Department for the Aging, 1993).

ETHNIC DIFFERENCES

Some informal accounts describe the Asian reluctance to involve the police by crime reporting (Kim, 1993). Similarly, an East Indian speaker on elder abuse in New York City's East Indian community (at the National Association of Social Worker World Assembly Conference in Washington, DC in July 1992) stated there was tremendous pressure on victims not to report this type of abuse to the police. The reason given was that members of new immigrant communities struggling for upward mobility do not want to publicize problems that may bring disgrace to their public image.

A recent study on the perceptions of elder abuse and help-seeking patterns among Black, White, and Asian (Korean) elderly women found evidence of ethnic differences in perceptions of abusive situations. Using written scenarios of potentially abusive family situations involving an elderly member, the researchers asked elderly subjects to rate them as abusive or non-abusive. Black subjects rated scenarios as abusive most often, followed by White subjects. Asian (Korean) subjects were the least likely to identify scenarios as reflecting elder abuse (Moon & Williams, 1993). While the study used a small sample and was confined to one Midwestern city, it suggests that perceptions of what constitutes an abusive situation may be culturally influenced and may in turn be another factor affecting reporting of abuse for specific ethnic groups.

SIGNIFICANCE OF EXAMINING STATED WILLINGNESS TO PROSECUTE BY ELDER ABUSE VICTIMS

At present, a significant gap exists in the literature on elder abuse and its relationship to the criminal justice system. This is in spite of the fact that many of the acts defined as elder abuse correspond to crimes as defined by the criminal justice system. The National Resource Center on Elder Abuse (NARCEA), in its noteworthy agenda setting report on elder abuse, identified the use of the criminal justice system as an intervention strategy in a key area where research is needed (NARCEA, 1991).

To begin to remedy this dearth of knowledge about the role of the criminal justice system and elder abuse, the present study was undertaken using as a data base a selection of complaint reports provided by the New York City Police Department (NYPD) on victims of crimes associated with elder abuse. The study examines complaint reports of elderly victims of abuse by offspring, with particular focus on victims' stated willingness or unwillingness to prosecute their abusers.

The underlying assumption in focusing on victims' willingness to prosecute is that—if in the affirmative—it is a positive outcome inasmuch as it provides a means of case finding through follow-up and may have a protective effect in discouraging future abuse episodes. It will also lead to the continuing involvement of the criminal justice system. Benefits include the opportunity to study the effect of this involvement as an intervention strategy in elder abuse, improved detection of abuse by police and increased awareness of elder abuse in the community. This information and awareness would be of value and interest to the community policing program, as well as advocates and service providers for the elderly, and could also serve to promote increased collaboration between community-based service programs for the elderly and local precincts.

A study of older adults who have filed complaints of abuse by family members has relevance for social work as well. First of all, it is assumed that many older clients who are victims of abuse by family members can benefit from involvement in the criminal justice system. However, considerable social work support may be necessary during this process either in encouraging and counseling an older client to consider this an option, and/or supporting and guiding the client through the process of prosecuting an abuser who is also a family member, or negotiating within the family or criminal court system for an order of protection.

In addition, police, community leaders, and service providers can benefit from a collaborative effort that leads to increased security and well-being of elderly community members and the community at large.

Information on ethnicity of victims and types of crimes likely to be committed against older persons by offspring can assist the community policing program and the aging service network to target preventive and outreach efforts more effectively (McElroy, Cosgove, & Sadd, 1993).

Knowing in advance which abused elders are likely to express a willingness to prosecute can be useful both to the social work practitioner and the attending police officer. Working as a team, the social worker and police officer can most effectively target interventions toward clients when there is some reasonable predictability of outcome.

Complaint reports filed by the NYPD on abuse incidents by or on behalf of crime victims are a valuable and—as noted—often overlooked source of information on elder abuse. They provide data on many of the variables that are considered significant to the understanding of elder abuse and how to address it. Descriptions of reported crimes on the complaint reports include inferences about the nature of the relationship between victim and abuser. Specifically, information captured on the complaint reports includes age, gender, ethnicity, living situation, and relationship of both victim and abuser.

Complaint reports also include types of offense (which are further described in a narrative remarks section), whether the victim self-reported the incident or it was reported by a witness, and in some cases include references made by a victim or onlooker about an abuser's alleged substance abuse or psychiatric problems. Finally, they identify whether the victim states willingness to prosecute, important information for case finding and follow-up purposes. In addition, some of the findings reported in the domestic violence literature suggest that prosecution can have a deterrent effect on future abuse (Sherman & Cohn, 1990).

Although complaint reports identify the precincts in which victims live, not all precincts are coterminous with community districts—from which census data are gathered on a number of variables, including economic and other demographic elements of the communities served by precincts. Therefore, this type of information is not accessible through analysis of complaint reports alone. However, examination of the other data available on complaint reports can increase the knowledge base for professionals working with older adults experiencing or at risk of abuse or exploitation by family members.

CHAPTER III

Research Methodology

As stated in Chapter I, the purpose of this research was to:

1. Develop a descriptive profile of elder abuse as reported to NYPD.

2. Expand the knowledge base of types of criminal offenses committed against elderly people by their offspring, and translate criminal justice terminology into categories of elder abuse already established by gerontologists, sociologists, social workers, and protective service for adults statutes.

3. Test the hypothesis that it is possible to predict, only using information obtainable from police complaint reports of elderly victims of domestic mistreatment who come to the attention of local law enforcement agencies, which elders will state willingness to prosecute their abusers at the time of the initial complaint.

4. Utilize the findings of the study to make recommendations to the law enforcement and social service communities regarding collaborative efforts that may be jointly undertaken to ensure the safety and quality of life of older community residents in Manhattan.

The stated purpose of the research was to obtain and analyze descriptive data on elder abuse as reported to law enforcement and test the hypothesis that it is possible to differentiate elder abuse victims who state willingness to prosecute to police when reporting a crime committed against them by offspring. To accomplish this, a survey was undertaken utilizing data obtained from complaint reports filed by the New York City Police Department (NYPD) in Manhattan during calendar year 1992.

Because original copies of complaint reports were utilized, available information permitted determining the initial decision of the elder victim as to whether to prosecute the abuser (perpetrator). This data source also contained narrative descriptions of the identified alleged crimes perpetrated against relatives aged 60 and older by offspring that permitted comparison of reported crimes with accepted definitions of elder abuse from the existing literature.

RELIABILITY AND VALIDITY OF DATA COLLECTION

Police have been trained in the preparation of complaint reports for victims of domestic violence as well as sensitized to the issued elder abuse (McQuillan, 1986; Plotkin, 1988). The complaint report form utilized by the NYPD is standardized and used as admissible court evidence. As noted, the reported crimes are categorized according to offenses as outlined in the penal law. Criteria for identifying them as reflective of elder abuse included: age of victim (60 years and above), relationship with abuser (offspring defined for the purpose of the study as all reports coded "3" for "child" by the reporting officer), and type of crime. A description of offenses used as match criteria for the purposes of this study is included in Chapter IV.

While this study sought to differentiate among victims based on their stated willingness to prosecute at initial contact with the police, it is possible that at a subsequent stage the elderly person will change his or her mind. Theoretically one could track the identified incidents of abuse through the criminal justice system to determine final outcome on those where the victims had initially declared themselves as willing to prosecute. Unfortunately this requires many more levels of approvals for release of information and raises serious confidentiality issues. Therefore, pursuing of cases beyond the initial complaint report was determined to be beyond the scope of the present study. NYPD confidentiality mandates precluded the researcher from learning the identities of victims and perpetrators in the study.

In order to track each incident through the criminal justice system, it would be necessary to rely on NYPD to blind code each report, forward to the reporting precinct where a detective would have to search the files and identify the outcome of a second contact with those victims declaring themselves willing to prosecute, then track (still using blind coding) that second group through family or criminal court, and/or the District Attorney's office. In addition, some reported offenses are not prosecutable (family dispute cases, for example), and other court records, where prosecution may have occurred, could be already sealed.

In the event that a follow-up study would become possible, all identified reports were selected from the borough of Manhattan. This is not only because Manhattan is a representative borough in terms of demographics of aging and ethnic/racial diversity, but also because of the Manhattan District Attorney's Office stated responsiveness to the issue of elder abuse: It contains a specialized unit for elder abuse-related crimes, and is represented on the New York City Elder Abuse Coalition. These factors suggested to the researcher that the present study would be most effective—in terms of generating useful information and in terms of potential for follow-up—if it remained focused on the borough of Manhattan.

The following variables were included in the study and the reasons for their inclusion noted. Variables are grouped as:

A. Characteristics of Victims Variables
B. Characteristics of Abusers Variables
C. Living Arrangements between Victim and Abuser Variable
D. Reporter of Abuse Variable
E. Type and Intensity of Abuse Variables
F. Victims' Stated Willingness to Prosecute Variable
G. Types of Elder Abuse Models That Differentiate Their Stated Willingness to Prosecute Offspring Abusers.

Variable groups A and B represent independent variables; variable groups C, D, and E represent intervening/structural variables; variable F is the outcome or criterion variable under study, and variable G represents two different types of elder abuse models.

A. *Victim Characteristics.* Age of victim. Rationale: Age of victim is correlated with impairment and dependency, with younger elder abuse victims (between the ages of 60 and 74 years) more likely to be financially independent of the abuser offspring, and older victims (age 75 years and above) more likely to suffer impairments and depend more on offspring for care and support.

Gender of victim. Rationale: A pilot study (Brownell, 1990) found that the gender of the abuser can influence the decision of the victim as to whether to express willingness to prosecute at the time the complaint is made to the police.

Race/ethnicity of victim. Rationale: While no studies have suggested that any one race/ethnicity shows more propensity for domestic violence than any other, Blacks are reported to utilize the criminal justice system in reporting domestic violence more often than other race/ethnicities (U.S. Department of Justice, 1984). As a result, there is an expectation that Black victims will be more likely to state willingness to prosecute their off-spring abusers than non-Black victims. *Note.* Because the study is examining offspring abuse, it is assumed that race/ethnicity of the victim will be the same as the abuser unless otherwise stated.

B. *Abuser Characteristics.* Age of abuser. Rationale: Younger abusers are more likely to be dependent on victims, whereas older abusers are more likely to be providing support and care to impaired older victims.

Gender of abuser. Rationale: The gender of the abuser may play a mediating role in a victim's decision to state willingness to prosecute, with victims generally more likely to state willingness to prosecute a male, but not female, abuser. Female off-spring have been identified as providing more of the instrumental tasks of caregiving, as opposed to male siblings (Stoller, Forster, & Duniho, 1992).

C. *Living Arrangements Between Victim and Abuser.* Living situation of victim. Rationale: Those victims living with the abuser may be less willing to prosecute than those not living with the abuser/perpetrator out of fear of retaliation or losing needed support.

D. *Reporter of Abuse.* Reporter of abuse to police. Rationale: The self-report victims may be more motivated or empowered to state willingness to prosecute than those victims for whom reports to the police were made by other parties. This is based on the self-reporting victims demonstrated initiative in making the report in the first place.

E. *Type/Intensity of Abuse.* Type of abuse (physical/ psychological/ financial). Rationale: The type of abuse may play a mediating role in a victim's decision to state willingness to prosecute. Victims of financial or psychological abuse may feel empowered to state willingness to prosecute once the police are contacted, while victims of physical abuse may feel too intimidated and fearful to state willingness to prosecute.

Intensity of abuse. Rationale: The intensity of the abuse may influence the victim's decision to express willingness to prosecute at time of complaint. Victims may feel less constrained from stating willingness to prosecute low intensity abuse—once it has been reported to the police, and more constrained from stating willingness to prosecute high intensity abuse. This may be because of fear of reprisal from the abuser, or—alternatively—concern about severity of punishment for the abuser, if convicted.

High intensity crimes are defined for the purposes of the study as rape, assault, menacing, attempted or actual grand larceny or robbery, and forgery. Low intensity crimes, for the purposes of this study, include harassment, criminal mischief, criminal trespassing, larceny, and petit larceny. Family disputes are not included as reflective of elder abuse, according to the definitions established for the study.

F. *Victims' Stated Willingness to Prosecute.* Willingness to prosecute (as reported in the complaints). Rationale: Victims' stated willingness to prosecute their off-spring abusers is an important outcome variable in that it determines whether follow-up will occur through the criminal justice system to the reported abuse situation.

G. *Types of Elder Abuse Victims that Differentiate Their Stated Willingness to Prosecute Offspring Abusers.* In addition to obtaining information on the variables listed above describing elder abuse as reflected in NYPD complaint reports for the defined time period (calendar year 1992) in Manhattan, the study was intended to determine if it were possible to categorize victims of abusive incidents according to two alternative models of elder abuse: the abuser dependency model and the caretaker stress model. These are included as constructed variables representing efforts to classify victims according to these two models of elder abuse.

1. *Abuser Dependency Model (Model A).* The profile of victims most likely to state willingness to prosecute at the time of the complaint report was hypothesized to reflect the abuser dependency model of abuse proposed by Karl Pillemer, based on the assumption that the victim—as the caretaker relative of the abuser—would not be as dependent on the abuser for care and support and therefore would feel fewer constraints about reporting abuse. As a result, it is further hypothesized that stated willingness to report lower level abuse would be associated with this profile.

2. *Caretaker Stress Model (Model B).* The profile of victims least likely to state unwillingness to prosecute at the time of the complaint report was hypothesized to reflect the caretaker stress model proposed by Suzanne Steinmetz. For abuse situations reflecting this model, victims are presumed to be more dependent on the abuser for care and as a result, more constrained from reporting the abuse and unwilling to prosecute even high level abuse.

DATA COLLECTION

The sources for data utilized in the study are complaint reports (PD 313-152 [Rev 3-88]-31) filed by NYPD in 1992 in Manhattan reflecting alleged offenses against people aged 60 years and above by offspring (identified for the purposes of this study as any perpetrator identified as "code 3—child" on the complaint report). Permission to obtain this information was granted by the Commissioner of NYPD at the request of the Human Resources Administration Commissioner (Appendix D).

A liaison was assigned from the NYPD Office of Management and Analysis Program (OMAP) to coordinate the NYPD response to the study. Permission for access to complaint reports was granted by the

NYPD legal division, based on the identification of data that must be withheld from the researcher in order to protect the confidentiality of victims and perpetrators (Appendix E).

OMAP staff wrote and ran a program to identify those complaint reports filed in 1992 in Manhattan that matched the criteria set forth by the researcher (described above). A request was made by the NYPD liaison to the file room (basement of One Police Plaza, the central office of NYPD) to pull the original copies of the complaint reports identified as reflecting the match criteria for inclusion in the study. The liaison then duplicated copies of all complaint reports pulled, deleted the data identified as confidential by the NYPD Legal Department, forwarded the duplicated copies to the researcher (keeping a set of copies without deletions in the event of follow-up questions), and returned the originals to the NYPD file room. Deleted data included names, birthdates (but not ages), street and apartment addresses of victims, perpetrators, witnesses, and names of reporters of incidents (if different from victim).

CODING OF DATA

The researcher coded all applicable information on data entry forms (Appendix F). Coding criteria are included on the data entry forms.

"Type of abuse" was coded based on an analysis of the identified offenses listed on the complaint reports in conjunction with a review of the narrative description of the abuse event as reported to the responding officer.

A critical feature of the study was to develop a classification schema for translating offenses as identified on and reported from complaint reports into categories of elder abuse developed and utilized by researchers from the fields of gerontology, sociology and social work. To address this, open ended statements were coded into nominal categories to examine the date gathered on the abuse variable.

Benefits of performing this analysis include enhanced ability to translate categories of offenses used by law enforcement agents into those used by elder abuse researchers to date, and to explore from two differing perspectives the impact of category and intensity of abuse on willingness to prosecute on the part of the victim. In addition, this allowed further exploration of associations between abuse and ethnicity and gender.

A frequently utilized classification schema for elder abuse is that developed by Wolf and Pillemer (1984). This includes active and passive neglect, physical abuse, financial abuse, and psychological abuse. Because not all reported offenses necessarily constitute "elder abuse," a category of "no abuse" was also included. As noted in Chapter I, the category of "neglect" was not used: New York State does not have a mandatory reporting system for elder abuse and neglect by a family member is not identified as a criminal offense in the New York Penal Code. In addition, some complaints were identified as "family disputes or offenses" and reflected family altercations where the older adult may have been a participant but not the target or victim of abuse.

Categories in the elder abuse literature that are captured through reports to law enforcement agencies include physical, financial, and psychological abuse. However, while some offenses fall clearly into one of these categories (rape or assault as physical abuse and larceny or forgery as financial abuse), others—such as harassment, menacing, and robbery—are not so clear-cut. This is because harassment or menacing can be reported as intended to annoy, intimidate, and distress (psychological abuse) or to obtain money or property (financial abuse). As noted, robbery, which on the surface would appear to represent financial abuse, can involve physical force against the identified victim as well.

In addition, both harassment and menacing, for example, can involve pushing, slapping or other forms of physical abuse. The difference between this and assault is related to the amount of injury sustained as defined by the victim. The difference between harassment or menacing with intent to obtain money or property and larceny or robbery is also the success or lack of it in obtaining the desired goal on the part of the abuser.

The United States Department of Justice provides guidelines for uniform crime reporting. Eight crimes are designated to compose the Uniform Crime Reports Crime (UCR) Index, based on their seriousness and frequency. They are murder and non-negligent manslaughter, forcible rape, robbery, aggravated assault, burglary, larceny-theft, motor-vehicle theft, and arson. Some of the offenses are not relevant for this study (with willingness to prosecute as the outcome of interest, murder and manslaughter become irrelevant, for example). In addition, many of the offenses committed against older people by offspring are not as serious in nature as those listed in the UCR, but nonetheless fall into established categories of elder abuse.

The UCR guidelines, however, offer some useful criteria for developing a classification schema of offenses listed on the complaint reports used in the study that can more effectively translate identified offenses into existing categories of elder abuse. The UCR counts as crimes all attempts as well as successfully completed crimes. As a result, harassment, menacing, criminal trespassing, and criminal mischief have been differentiated into subcategories reflecting physical, financial, and psychological abuse, based on descriptions of the incident as reported by the victim on the complaint report. One exception is threats of harm that were not carried out: These were categorized as psychological as opposed to physical abuse. Unsuccessful efforts to obtain money, property or possessions from a victim were categorized as financial abuse, however, as the motivation was assumed to be one of acquisition of money or property and not necessarily harassment.

If more than one index offense occurs during a single incident, only the most serious is reported in the UCR program and included in the Crime Index total (U.S. Department of Justice, 1981). This system has been followed, with each complaint report coded as representing only the most serious form of reported abuse, regardless of whether multiple types of abuse were identified.

Using the criteria developed for the UCR as a guide, physical abuse was identified as more serious than other forms of abuse, and financial as more serious than psychological abuse in the absence of reported physical abuse. For example, a complaint report reflecting slapping, attempts to steal property, and yelling to intimidate the victim would be coded as physical abuse. Attempted or actual stealing of money or property and verbal abuse would be coded as financial abuse. Verbal abuse and/or threats (without actual use of physical force or a weapon) would be coded as psychological abuse.

A representative sampling of these narratives illustrating the identified offenses and their subsets is included in Chapter IV. The purposes of the recoding of the offenses listed on the crime report were three-fold:

1. To provide improved descriptive data for the study.
2. To facilitate comparison with existing data from the elder abuse literature.
3. To allow for refining the relationship between stated willingness to prosecute and alleged offense, as well as relating type (category) and intensity of offense to hypothesized explanatory models of abuse.

TYPES OF OFFENSES

Following is a listing of recorded offenses against elderly victims by offspring identified in the complaint reports provided by the NYPD for the study.

Under the abuse categories (physical, financial and psychological), the researcher included:

1. Harassment/physical (contact, shoving, throwing objects at victim).
2. Harassment/financial (demands for money, property).
3. Harassment/psychological (threats, stalking, making unwanted demands, banging on door and calling repeatedly on the telephone after being asked not to by the victim).
4. Criminal Trespass/psychological (entering victim's living residence without permission and refusing to leave).
5. Criminal Mischief/financial (destroying property in efforts to intimidate victim to give abuser money or property).
6. Menacing/physical (hitting or pushing victim in addition to threatening with gun, knife and/or other object with the potential to inflict bodily harm).
7. Menacing/financial (threatening victim with object[s] that have the potential for inflicting bodily harm for the purpose of obtaining money or property from the victim).

8. Menacing/psychological (threatening victim with object[s] that have the potential for inflicting bodily harm for the purpose of intimidating or harassing the victim).
9. Assault, Third Degree/physical (inflicting injury on victim with body of abuser; victim requires medical attention).
10. Assault, Second Degree/physical (inflicting injury on victim that is potentially life threatening; victim requires medical attention).
11. Assault, First Degree/Physical (using a weapon, inflicts injury on victim that requires medical attention and is life-threatening).
12. Rape/physical (forcefully performs sexual acts on victim without victim's consent).
13. Petit Larceny/financial (takes money or property with value of $150 or less without victims' consent).
14. Larceny (takes money or property without victim's consent: value not determined at time complaint was filed).
15. Attempted Grand Larceny/financial (attempts to take money or property without victim's consent; value is in excess of $150).
16. Grand Larceny/financial (takes victim's money or property without consent; value is in excess of $150).
17. Attempted and Actual Robbery/physical (forcibly removes money or property from victim's person, inflicting injury in the process).
18. Robbery/financial (forcibly removes money or property from victim's person; injuries not sustained).
19. Forgery/financial (signs victim's name to documents without permission or authorization for the purpose of stealing money or property from victim).

Family Disputes were excluded as they were not defined as elder abuse situations for the purpose of the study. An analysis of reported offenses involving a family member 60 years of age and older revealed this as a category of offense that reflected arguments among family members where it was not possible to identify any specific victim, although a family member aged at least 60 years was involved in the dispute along with off-spring.

In addition, baseline categories of offenses were recategorized as high/low abuse, based on criteria from the UCR classification. Felonies are rated as high levels of abuse, while in most instances violation and misdemeanor-level offenses are rated as low levels of abuse, based on the type of offense identified by the reporting officer in conjunction with a content analysis of the descriptive paragraph on the complaint report.

Exceptions were made for menacing and assault in the third degree, based on an analysis of narrative descriptions of the abuse situations reflected in the complaint reports. Menacing (a class A misdemeanor unless the perpetrator had been convicted of a similar offense in the past 10 years) was classified for the purposes of this study as a high intensity form of abuse. Assault in the third degree, another class A misdemeanor was also classified in this study as a high intensity form of abuse.

The high/low categories cut across the categories of physical/financial/psychological abuse, but permitted further analysis of victims' willingness to prosecute under differing conditions of abuse.

Included under high level abuse were the categories of menacing (physical, financial, and psychological), assaults 3, 2, and 1, rape, attempted and actual grand larceny, attempted and actual robbery and forgery. Included under low level abuse were harassment (physical, financial and psychological), criminal trespassing, criminal mischief, larceny and petit larceny.

STUDY SAMPLE

As noted above, the study sample provided by the NYPD reflected complainants aged 60 years and above reporting alleged crimes committed against them by offspring (code 3—"Child"—on the complaint reports). These complaints were filed in the borough of Manhattan during calendar year 1992 in all 21 precincts (including Manhattan South and Manhattan North). Using the match criteria submitted to NYPD by the researcher, a 100% sample was drawn.

As a result, this study reflects the universe of complaint reports reflecting the criteria for elder abuse filed in Manhattan in 1992. This allows for limited generalizability as it is specific to the borough of Manhattan during the sample year. However, the findings are useful in suggesting areas for further study, and for providing a baseline of comparison with data from other boroughs of New York City and from law enforcement agencies in other metropolitan areas.

RELIABILITY/VALIDITY

The study utilized data collected on a standardized reporting form utilized by all NYPD police in capturing reports of alleged crimes. As noted, all police are trained to use the reporting form in a uniform manner, and it is admissible as a court document. This attests to the reliability and validity of the information contained in the complaint reports.

The researcher reviewed and coded all information from the complaint reports as part of the study. This further strengthens the reliability of the data collection and coding process.

PLAN OF ANALYSIS

The goal of the analysis was to identify which if any of the selected variables are significant in differentiating among victims based on their stated willingness to prosecute the abuser (perpetrator). In addition, the study attempted to identify a profile, or cluster, of characteristics that can predict which reports will result in the desired outcome of a complaint to the police on elder abuse: willingness on the part of the victim to prosecute the abuser (perpetrator). To further confirm or explore associations identified by the bivariate analyses, multivariate analyses were employed. Finally, there was an effort to determine whether the data collected on the abuse incidents permitted categorizing victims according to explanatory models of elder abuse as proposed by Pillemer and Steinmetz.

The statistical analysis of the data collected by this survey was limited by the nature of the variables under examination. Except for age, all identified variables—independent, intervening (structural), and dependent—are nominal and, in most instances, dichotomous. This limited the analysis primarily to non-parametric statistical tests; these are not considered as powerful or robust as parametric procedures, but are commonly used to test hypotheses in the social sciences where variables do not always meet the more rigorous criteria for parametric tests or analyses (Hinkle, Wiersma, & Jurs, 1988).

DESCRIPTIVE STATISTICS

Prior to employing any of the more sophisticated, hypothesis-testing statistical techniques in analyzing the data, an analysis of descriptive information on the sample was undertaken. This included demographic data and simple frequency distributions of the variables selected for analysis. The results of this descriptive level of analysis are included in Chapter IV.

The findings from the analytic procedures intended to test the study hypotheses are included in Chapter V. A review of these analytic procedures is included here:

BIVARIATE ANALYSIS: CHI SQUARE (FOR INDEPENDENCE/ASSOCIATION)

The first non-parametric procedure to be used as a test of association is that of the chi square. This procedure was used to compare the observed frequencies of occurrence with theoretical or expected frequencies (Hinkle et. al., 1988). Based on the sample of complaint reports examined in the study, the following questions are addressed: Is there a significant association between a victim's stated willingness to prosecute and a victim's age? Are elderly men more likely than elderly women to state willingness to prosecute their abusers? What if any is the association between victims' race/ethnicity and stated willingness to prosecute their offspring abuser? Does the age or gender of the abuser influence a victims's stated willingness to prosecute? Does the living situation between abuser and victim influence a victim's stated willingness to prosecute? Is a victim who self-reports the abuse to the police more likely to state willingness to prosecute the abuser than a victim whose abuse is reported by a third party? What is the relationship between category of abuse and a victim's stated willingness to prosecute the abuser? How does intensity of abuse influence a victim's decision to state willingness to prosecute?

MULTIVARIATE ANALYSIS: LOGISTIC REGRESSION

When examining multiple nominal variables, the probability of an individual belonging to a category of interest (dependent variable) can be assessed using logistic regression analysis (Kachigan, 1986). Logistic regression analysis was employed to examine the relationship between the dichotomous dependent variable (stated willingness to prosecute at time of reported complaint), and the explanatory (independent—or predictor) and intervening variables.

This form of statistical analysis was utilized to determine if it were possible to predict membership of a given elder abuse victim in the group stating willingness to prosecute and—if so—which variables have the greatest predictive value. This is intended to answer the research question of whether victims coming to the attention of the NYPD can be categorized according to one of two hypothesized models of elder abuse: the abuser dependency model and the caretaker stress model, based on the information in police complaint reports reflecting elder abuse situations.

As noted, the premise of this phase of the analysis is that the development of a profile of abuse with predictive power could be useful in identifying elderly victims who could benefit from targeted intervention by social work/police teams. The goal of the interventions would be to ensure optimal protection and safety of victims.

MULTIVARIATE ANALYSIS: CLASSIFICATION AND REGRESSION TREES (CART)

The next form of statistical analysis employed is a non-parametric technique for analyzing nominal data (SYSTAT, 1992). It utilizes the concept of branching variables based on an analysis of how much the variables contribute to an understanding of the phenomenon under examination (in this case, elder abuse as reported to the NYPD in Manhattan in 1992). It is intended to strengthen understanding of the predictive value of variables identified as explanatory of a given phenomenon.

The purpose of utilizing this procedure was to verify and clarify the results of the logistic regression. As noted, these regression techniques were utilized to identify multiple variables that were predictive of elder abuse victims' stated willingness to prosecute their abusers (perpetrators) at the time of the initial report of abuse to the police. In addition, they were utilized in an effort to determine which variables under analysis had the greatest predictive value in understanding elder abuse as reflected in the study sample.

CHAPTER IV

Description of the Sample

The purpose of this chapter is to describe the sample of complaint reports representing elder abuse situations reported to the NYPD during 1992 in Manhattan. This comprises 314 complaint reports, of which 19 were identified as "family dispute cases" but not "elder abuse" in that the older person identified in the report appeared to be a participant in a family dispute but not a target of abuse. The family dispute cases were eliminated from the sample and were not analyzed in this study.

The 295 complaint reports that remained after eliminating the family dispute cases represented the universe of incidents that came to the attention of NYPD defined as elder abuse based on the match criteria submitted by the researcher:

1. Victim (complainant) 60 years of age or older.
2. Abuser (perpetrator) related to victim as offspring (coded as 3—child) by the attending officer at the time the complaint was made.
3. Victim resides in Manhattan and complaint was filed with a police precinct in Manhattan during calendar year 1992.
4. Abuse (alleged crime) reflects one of three categories of elder abuse as defined in the literature (psychological, physical, or financial). Complaint reports reflecting abuse included all those but ones identified as "family dispute" cases, which totaled 19 out of the universe of 314. These were separated out from the sample by the researcher based on the narrative descriptions that suggested the older person involved was not

a victim but rather a participant in the dispute. They also do not fit the minimum for classification as a crime and therefore should not be included as part of the sample of elder abuse complaint reports.

DESCRIPTION OF COMPLAINT REPORTS REFLECTING ELDER ABUSE

There were 295 complaint reports identified by NYPD that reflected elder abuse as defined by the criteria that a person aged 60 years of age or above was the victim of physical, psychological, or financial abuse by an offspring. Of these, 238 contained information on willingness to prosecute—which was the outcome variable examined by the study.

A comparison with the larger sample of 295 complaint reports showed that the 238 complaint reports used in the study were proportionally similar to the larger sample and as a result were not reflective of selection bias. For a detailed description of the sample of the 295 cases (of which the 238 used in the study was a subsample), see Appendix H. A description of the sample of 238 complaint reports is provided below. Tables 2 through 8 include data on each of the study variables for the sample of 238 abuse reports with information on victims' stated willingness to prosecute.

Description of Elder Abuse Victims (Table 2)

The ages of the victims in the 238 sample ranged from 60 to 93 years of age, with a mean age of 69 and a standard deviation of 7. One hundred ninety-five (82%) of the sample were in the young-old age group (60 to 74 years of age) and 43 (18%) were in the old-old age group (75 years of age and older). The victims in the sample were predominately female (176 or 74%) as opposed to male (62 or 26%). Because the sample reflects offspring abuse, it is assumed that both victim and abuser are the same race/ethnicity. The sample included 49 (21%) Whites, 131 or 55% Blacks, 1 or .4% Asian, and 57 or 24% Hispanic victims/abusers. *Note*: Race/ethnic categories reflect those used in police complaint reports. Native American (the fifth category) was dropped as no offenses reflecting elder abuse based on the study criteria were reported to the NYPD in Manhattan in 1992. For purposes of consistency, these categories are used throughout the study in discussions of race/ethnicity and elder abuse.

Table 2: Description of Sample Population (238 Complaint Reports):

Victim Characteristics	N	%
Age (average)	69	238100
(SD)	7	
Age group		
60-74 years (young-old)	195	82
75 years + (old-old)	43	18
Gender		
Female	176	74
Male	62	26
Race/ethnicity		
White	49	21
Black	131	55
Hispanic	57	24
Asian	1	< 1

Description of Abusers (Table 3)

The age of the abusers ranged from 13 to 69 years of age. The mean age of the abusers was 34 years and the standard deviation was 10. The abusers in the sample were predominately male (188 or 79% male as opposed to 50 or 21% female). Abusers of elders in the sample included 186 (78%) sons, 45 (19%) daughters, 1 (.4%) stepson, 1 (.4%) stepdaughter, 4 (2%) grandsons, and 1 (.4%) granddaughter.

The majority of abuse reports did not include information on substance abuse by abuser (201 or 84%). A total of 37 (16%) quoted the reporter that the abuser was a substance abuser: Substances identified included both illegal drugs and alcohol.

Living Arrangements Between Victims and Abusers (Table 4)

The majority of the victims lived with their abusers: One hundred twenty-five (53%) lived with their abusers as opposed to 100 (42%) who did not. Of the 238 complaint reports studied, 13 (6%) did not include information on living arrangements between victims and abusers.

Table 3: Abuser Characteristics

	N	%
Abuser age (average)	34	238100
(*SD*)	10	
Abuser gender		
Female	50	21
Male	188	79
Relation to victim:		
Son	186	78
Daughter	45	19
Stepson	1	< 1
Stepdaughter	1	< 1
Grandson	4	2
Granddaughter	1	< 1
Abuser substance abuse:		
Yes	37	16
No information	201	84

Table 4: Living Arrangements Between Victim and Abuser

	N	%
Live together	125	53
Live apart	100	42
No information	13	5

Who Reported Crime to Police (Table 5)

The majority of the victims reported the abuse to the police themselves (212 or 89% as opposed to 26 or 11% who did not).

Table 5: Reporter to Police

	N	%
Victim reported	212	89
Other reported	26	11

Willingness to Prosecute (Table 6)

Stated willingness to prosecute is important to this study because for those stating in the affirmative, there is a second contact by the precinct to which the victim reported the abuse incident. The second contact provides an opportunity for case tracking.

The majority of elder abuse victims in the sample stated willingness to prosecute (176 or 74%) as opposed to unwillingness to prosecute (62 or 26%). Of the 72 victims who experienced high level abuse, 63 or 88% stated willingness to prosecute; of 166 victims who experienced low level abuse, 113 or 68% stated willingness to prosecute.

Table 6: Victims' Stated Willingness to Prosecute

	N	%
Yes	176	74
No	62	26

Family Crimes Against the Elderly

Type of Abuse

Based on the categories defined by Pillemer and Wolf (physical, financial, and psychological), types of abuse reflected in the complaint reports reviewed in the study included 73 (31%) reports of physical abuse, 80 (34%) reports of financial abuse and 85 (36%) psychological abuse. Table 7 shows the breakdown of offenses by category of abuse.

Table 7: Breakdown of Offenses by Category of Abuse

	N	%
Physical abuse	73	30.7
Assault 1	1	< 1.0
Rape	1	< 1.0
Assault 2	8	3.4
Assault 3	27	11.3
Attempted/actual robbery physical	3	1.3
Menacing/physical	3	1.3
Harassment/physical	30	12.6
Financial abuse	80	33.6
Grand larceny	15	6.3
Robbery/financial	4	1.7
Attempted grand larceny	1	< 1.0
Larceny	5	2.1
Forgery	1	< 1.0
Menacing/financial	1	< 1.0
Criminal mischief/financial	3	1.3
Petit larceny	32	13.4
Harassment/financial	18	7.6
Psychological abuse	85	35.7
Menacing/psychological	7	2.9
Criminal trespass/psychological	1	< 1.0
Harassment/psychological	77	32.4

Note. Offenses are listed as a percentage of universe, not category of abuse.

Intensity of Abuse

Based on the classification scheme adapted from the Uniform Crime Report, the offenses reflected in the sample were recoded into low and high intensity abuse. Low intensity abuse was recorded in 166 (70%) of the complaint reports and high intensity abuse was recorded in 72 (30%) of the sample complaint reports. The breakdown of high and low intensity offenses are shown below (Tables 8 and 9).

Table 8: Breakdown of High Intensity Abuse

High Intensity	N	%
Total	72	30.0
Physical	43	
Assault 1	1	< 1.0
Rape	1	< 1.0
Assault 2	8	3.4
Assault 3	27	11.3
Attempted/actual robbery/		
physical	3	1.3
Menacing/physical	3	1.3
Financial	22	
Grand larceny	15	6.3
Attempted grand larceny	1	< 1.0
Robbery/financial	4	1.7
Forgery	1	< 1.0
Menacing/financial	1	< 1.0
Psychological	7	
Menacing/psychological	7	2.9

Table 9: Breakdown of Low Intensity Offenses

Low Intensity	N	%
Total	166	70.0
Physical	30	
Harassment/physical	30	12.6
Financial		
Criminal mischief	3	1.3
Petit larceny	32	13.4
Harassment	18	7.6
Psychological	78	
Criminal trespass/		
psychological	1	< 1.0
Harassment/psychological	77	32.4

PRECINCTS REPORTING

The 10 (out of 21) highest ranking police precincts reporting abuse cases included precincts 23 (36), 32 (35), 28 (25), 24 (21), 25 (21), 30 (19), 34 (16), 14 (17), and 7 and 9 (both 10). All of the above precincts with the exception of 7 and 9 are located in upper Manhattan, with four of the top five located in Harlem; 7 and 9 are located in the Lower East Side of Manhattan. A chart listing precincts with number of elder abuse reports received is included here (Table 10). In addition, a map of precincts covering Manhattan is appended (Appendix G).

    Because police precincts become coterminous with community districts (by which census data are reported) only above 59 Street, and NYPD confidentiality mandates precluded providing information on complainants by zip code, little information regarding socioeconomic status of communities covered by precincts can be extrapolated. Some citywide data on economic status of older New Yorkers by ethnicity are available, however.

There is a striking difference in poverty status among White, Black and Hispanic older New Yorkers. According to a recent study of the elderly in New York, White elderly had the lowest proportion (13%) at or below poverty, Black elderly were next at 35% at or below poverty, and Hispanic elderly experienced the most poverty, with 57% at or below the poverty level (Cantor, 1993). It should be noted that these are citywide averages and do not necessarily reflect the economic status of victims included in this study.

Table 10: Breakdown of Complaint Reports by Precinct: Number (Percentage) Complaint Reports

Precinct	n	%
1/2: Tribeca/Wall Street	2	< 1.0
5: Chinatown/Little Italy	1	< 1.0
6: Greenwich Village	1	< 1.0
7: Lower East Side	10	4.2
9: East Village	10	4.2
10: Chelsea	2	< 1.0
13: Gramercy	2	< 1.0
14: Midtown South	3	1.3
17: Midtown	1	< 1.0
18: Midtown North	8	3.4
19: East Side	14	5.9
20: West Side	5	2.1
23: Upper East Side	36	15.1
24: Upper West Side	21	8.8
25: East Harlem	21	8.8
26: Morningside Heights	6	2.5
28: Central Harlem	25	10.5
30: Harlem (by RSD)	19	8.0
32: Harlem (North)	35	14.7
34: Washington Heights	16	6.7
Total	238	100.0

Reporting by ethnicity appears to roughly correlate with the ethnic make-up of the neighborhoods from which reports are made. As noted, Blacks tend to report more instances of domestic violence to law enforcement agencies more often than other ethnic/racial groups. This could explain the higher percentage of reporting in those neighborhoods (such as Harlem) in which residents are primarily Black.

SAMPLE POPULATION OF ELDERLY VICTIMS AS COMPARED WITH BOROUGHWIDE AND CITYWIDE POPULATIONS OVER 60 YEARS OF AGE ON SELECTED VARIABLES DISCUSSED ABOVE

As noted in Chapter III, the sample for the study included the universe of elder mistreatment complaints filed with the New York City Police Department in 1992. As such, it has limited generalizability beyond a description of that universe. In order to assess the proportional relationship between the study population and boroughwide and citywide populations on selected demographic variables examined in the study, however, an analysis was undertaken that compared the sample population with borough and citywide data from the 1990 census. This analysis compared the sample of 238 with borough and citywide data on gender, race/ethnicity and proportion of the over-60 population.

The results of that analysis are included here (Table 11). Manhattan is shown to be a representative borough based on the proportional analysis of gender, age, and race/ethnicity (with the exception of the Asian elderly population, which is overrepresented in Manhattan). However, the study population of abuse victims, compared with Manhattan demographics on these variables, appears disproportionately Black and "young-old" (aged 60 to 74 years). The gender breakdown of the victims for the sample population is 74% female and 26% male. This is as compared with 60% females and 40% males 60 years of age and older residing in Manhattan during the last census (1990). As large as the discrepancy is between male and female elder abuse victims in the sample, proportionally it is not statistically different from that of Manhattan or New York City (at the .07 level).

The ethnic breakdown of elder abuse victims in the study is 21% White, 55% Black, 24% Hispanic, and .4% Asian. This is compared to the demographic breakdown in Manhattan of 58% White, 18% Black, 17% Hispanic and 6% Asian residents age 60 years and above. In the sample population, 82% victims were age 60 to 74 years and 18% were age 75 years and above. This is compared to 66% age 60 to 74 years and 34% age 75 and above for Manhattan residents.

Table 11: Comparison Among Study Population, Manhattan, and Citywide Demographics for Selected Variables

Variables for Ages 60+	Study Sample (238)		Manhattan [a]		Citywide[a]	
	N	%	*N*	%	*N*	%
Totals	238	100	264,789	100	1,278,105	100
Gender						
Female		74		60		61
Male		26		40		39
Race/ ethnicity						
Black		55		18		18
White		21		58		65
Hispanic		24		17		13
Asian		<1		6		4
Age categories						
60-74 years		82		66		67
75 years+		18		34		33

[a]From New York City Department for the Aging (1993).

The study population is drawn from reports made in 1992 and information on borough and citywide demographics is drawn from the 1990 census. In addition, the study population reflects the universe of police complaint reports for 1992. As a result, it is not possible to generalize from these findings. Nonetheless, it is suggestive of the need for further research on these discrepancies and their possible implications.

NARRATIVE DESCRIPTIONS OF ABUSE AS REFLECTED IN COMPLAINT REPORTS

In order to give a richer sense of the nature of the alleged crimes reflected in above abuse groups, included here are excerpts from the narrative descriptions included in the complaint reports. The descriptions are organized according to category of abuse, ranging from physical to financial to psychological, and—within each category—from high intensity to low intensity. They were selected as representative of each type of reported offense.

According to the classification scheme used for the content analysis, any reported offense that includes physical abuse in the narrative description is categorized as "physical," regardless of whether it may also include actions on the part of the abuser reflecting financial and/or psychological abuse. Similarly, abuse situations reflecting both financial and psychological abuse (in the absence of reported physical abuse) are classified as financial. Reported abuse that does not include mention of either physical or financial abuse is classified as psychological abuse.

Within each category of abuse (physical, financial, and psychological), abuse incidents are further classified as high intensity or low intensity. Listed below are representative descriptions of abuse organized according to category of abuse, and—within each category—intensity of abuse (from high intensity to low intensity).

Physical Abuse (High Intensity)

Assault, First Degree.

> Complainant was in the hospital. She had suffered multiple injuries to her head and body. Complainant seemed confused about some facts. However, her doctor stated she had suffered a massive blow to the side of the head, and could be causing this confusion. Complainant states her son, daughter, and daughter's friend had held

her prisoner for the past several days. They stated they would kill her
if she left and beat her for no reason.

The 66-year-old female victim stated an unwillingness to press charges
against her son and other abusers (perpetrators) with whom she stated
she resided.

Rape.

Victim states above perp (son) entered her bedroom, pulled off the
covers and stated: "I'm going to fuck you." Complainant tried to
resist but the perp pulled her hair and punched her in the face. Perp
then forcibly held complainant down on the bed and penetrated her
vagina with his penis. Perp also stated that "if you go to the police
something will happen to you."

The 64-year-old victim stated a willingness to prosecute her 38-year-old
son, with whom she lived.

Assault, Second Degree.

Complainant presently at hospital and is being treated for burn
wounds to her legs and arms and for a possible broken hip. The
home attendant, who is also a witness, states that upon arrival for
work she observed the perp (son) strike the victim about her face
three times. . . . The manager of the building states they have had
many complaints of noise from victim's apartment.

The 88-year-old female victim refused to speak to police at the time the
complaint was filed; the home attendant served as witness. The abuser,
the 60-year-old son, was identified as residing with the victim.

Assault, Third Degree.

Complainant states (son) threw victim to ground, covered her face
with pillow and attempted to suffocate her. He lifted the pillow,
looked at victim and stated: "You're still alive," then again placed
pillow on victims' face.

The 61-year-old female victim stated a willingness to prosecute her 33-year-old son, with whom she lived.

Attempted/Actual Robbery.

Complainant stated that above perp (son) broke into apartment, punched complainant about the body and removed the above listed property (valuable watch set with precious stones). Perp then fled in unknown direction.

The 67-year-old female victim stated a willingness to prosecute her 22-year-old son.

Menacing, physical.

Victim states that the above perp (son) said: "Let me in, I need money." Then proceeded to place hand in door. Victim opened door and perp attacked victim by punching him and menacing him with a box cutter and scissors. Victim also states that perp said: "I'm going to kill you."

The 77-year-old male victim stated a willingness to prosecute his 20-year-old son, with whom he did not reside.

Physical Abuse (Low Intensity)

Harassment, physical.

Both complainant and witness state that the perp [victim's son] did yell at and push complainant, resulting in no physical injury, but causing said complainant to be alarmed.

The responding officer advised the victim (a 62-year-old woman) and her daughter (witness) how to obtain an Order of Protection against her 32-year-old son, and issued her a Crime Victim's Service Agency Card. Victim and abuser were identified as living together.

Financial Abuse (High Intensity)

Grand Larceny.

> Complainant and reporter (daughter) present as she states that perp fully [identified] above and who is her son entered her apartment and took stocks and bonds in the amount of $54,000 without complainant or reporter['s] permission or authority. The stocks and bonds are in complainant and reporter's names.

The 89-year-old female victim stated she was willing to prosecute her 55-year-old son, with whom she did not reside.

Forgery.

> Complainant reports that [the] above perp (his son) has forged his signature on above checks totalling $1,500 and did cash them without his permission or authority to do so.

The 60-year-old male victim stated a willingness to prosecute his 27-year-old son, with whom he lived.

Robbery.

> Victim states perp (son) came to his door and repeatedly banged on the door. The parents had an order of protection stating that he was not to come to his parents' residence and not to harass them. The father reluctantly let him in and then perp threatened father with bodily harm to give him $80 for drugs.

The 84-year-old father stated willingness to prosecute his 29-year-old son.

Attempted Grand Larceny.

> Perp (son) called complainant/victim and stated he wanted $50. If she didn't give him [the] money, he was going to kill her. Undersigned list[en]ed to telephone threat. Canvass of area proved to be negative.

The 73-year-old female victim stated a willingness to prosecute her 34-year-old son, with whom she did not reside.

Menacing, financial.

> Complainant states that her children frequently ask her to have her apartment to sell drugs. Complainant states her daughter is the one who purchases drugs to give to her brother to sell. Daughter is also a drug dealer. Complainant states they have weapons and threaten their mother, stating: "Any kind of accident can happen to you."

The 63-year-old female victim expressed willingness to prosecute her daughter, with whom stated she did not live.

Financial Abuse (Low Intensity)

Criminal Mischief/financial.

> Complainant stated that the above named perp the son of complainant's common law wife did cause damage to the telephone wires and did alarm and verbally abuse them arguing with them in search for money. Complainant and spouse [are] both senior citizens [and] are fearful of their son. Complainant was referred to Family Court for Order of Protection.

The victim, a 79-year-old man, stated a willingness to prosecute his common-law wife's 18-year-old son, with whom they did not live.

Larceny.

> Victim states perp (daughter) came to visit and removed from apartment without permission set of sterling silverware and a blanket (value to be determined). Perp is a known crack addict, according to victim.

The victim, a 65-year-old woman, stated willingness to prosecute her 37-year-old daughter, with whom she does not reside.

Petit Larceny.

> Victim states she invited her son in for dinner. When she turned her back, son took property [a clock radio] and fled. Victim states son has a drug problem.

The 68-year-old female victim stated a willingness to prosecute her son, with whom she did not reside.

Harassment, financial.

> Victim states that his son attempted to kick down his apartment door and demanded to be let in. Perp demanded $10,000 to leave father alone. Son threatened to "go all the way" if father didn't let him in. As son departed he stated he was "getting a gun" and would return. Son has made threats in the past and is an alleged crack abuser.

The victim, a 66-year-old man, was referred to Family Court for an Order of Protection against his 28-year-old son. The father and son were identified as not living together.

Psychological Abuse (High Intensity)

Menacing.

> Above complainant states she had a verbal dispute with perp (her son) at which time perp holding knife in hand said to complainant that he was going to cut her up into little pieces. Referred to Family Court for Order of Protection.

The victim, a 72-year-old woman, stated a willingness to prosecute her 32-year-old son, with whom she resided.

Psychological Abuse (Low Intensity)

Criminal Trespassing.

> Complainant states above listed perp who is her adopted son did enter living room window without permission or authority and upon several requests by complainant to leave. Complainant further states perp

> (son) does not reside at location and had not resided there for some
> time. Complainant states no property was removed or damaged.

The victim, a 60-year-old woman, stated a willingness to prosecute her
38-year-old son.

Harassment, psychological.

> Victim states perp (son) has been constantly harassing victim but perp
> flees when police respond. Victim informed by neighbor that perp
> told her he was going to kill his mother (victim). Victim is in fear of
> her life—son is an alcoholic, drug user, and was recently released
> from prison (on parole).

The complaint report identified the victim, a 73-year-old woman, as
willing to prosecute her 39-year-old son and stated "victim will report
to District Attorney's office on 125th Street today." Victim and abuser
were identified as not living together.

Family Dispute Case Description (Example)

Family offense or family dispute cases are sometimes included as elder
abuse cases when reported by the police in complaint reports. Although
not analyzed as part of this study, a representative example is provided
here. The purpose is to provide a contrast between this type of
complaint and those categorized as elder abuse cases in this study. The
family dispute cases were reported as altercations, sometimes of long
duration and usually over a specific issue or problem. An example from
the complaint reports includes:

> Complainant states [she and] her daughter were having an argument
> about mother's going out, because [the building] super[intendent] was
> coming to [fix] the toilet bowl.

(This is from a complaint made by a 76-year-old woman; the age of the
daughter was missing from the report. The officer taking the complaint
made a referral for family counseling.)

As noted, this study examines only those complaint reports defined as "elder abuse" situations, based on the criteria defined earlier.

CHAPTER V

Description of Findings

The purpose of this chapter is to describe the results of testing the hypothesis that by knowing certain information about an elder abuse victim living in Manhattan for whom a complaint report was filed with NYPD in 1992, it is possible to predict which victim will state willingness to prosecute at the time of filing a complaint report. This presumes that the characteristics of the victim under examination are significantly associated with the victims's stated willingness to prosecute his or her abuser. For the purposes of this study the abuser is an offspring: As noted in Chapter IV, stepchildren and grandchildren in the study population are included as offspring.

In addition, it presumes that these characteristics will cluster together in a profile that will allow prediction as to whether the victim is likely to state willingness to prosecute at the time of the filing of a complaint with the police regarding the experience of abuse by an offspring. The hypothesized profiles of victims who are likely to state willingness or unwillingness to prosecute at the time of filing a police report on experiencing abuse by an offspring are developed based on whether they reflect the abuse dependency model of elder abuse (Pillemer), or the caretaker stress model of elder abuse (Steinmetz). Those cases identified as reflecting the abuser dependency (Pillemer) model are hypothesized to show a high probability of stating willingness to prosecute, and those reflecting the caretaker stress (Steinmetz) model are hypothesized to show a high probability of stating unwillingness to prosecute the abuser.

HYPOTHESES/RESEARCH QUESTIONS

This analysis is based on a series of research questions. These include:

1. What is the relationship of victims' age to victims' stated willingness to prosecute the abuser offspring?
2. What is the relationship between victims' gender and stated willingness to prosecute their offspring abusers?
3. What is the relationship of race/ethnicity to victims' stated willingness to prosecute the abuser offspring?
4. What is the relationship of abusers' ages to victims' stated willingness to prosecute the abuser offspring?
5. What is the relationship between victims' stated willingness to prosecute and gender of abuser?
6. What is the relationship between victims' stated willingness to prosecute and the living arrangement between the abuser and the victim?
7. Is an elder abuse victim more likely to state willingness to prosecute his or her abuser if he or she has self-reported the abuse to the police?
8. What is the relationship of category of abuse (financial, physical, or psychological) to victims' stated willingness to victims' stated willingness to prosecute their abuser offspring?
9. What is the relationship between high/low intensity of abuse and victims' stated willingness to prosecute the abuser offspring?
10. Does the profile of a victim who states *willingness* to prosecute the abuser conforms to that hypothesized to match the abuser dependency model of elder abuse? Characteristics include a victim who is younger (60 to 74 years), male, and Black, whose abuser is younger, also male (son), and is a perpetrator of low level financial or psychological abuse. In

this model, the victim and abuser live apart and the victim has self-reported the abuse to the police.

11. Does the profile of a victim who states *unwillingness* to prosecute the abuser conform to that hypothesized to match the caretaker stress model of elder abuse? Characteristics include an abuser who is older (75 years and above), female, and White. The abuser is also older (above the mean age for group), female (daughter), and perpetrator of high level physical abuse. In this model, the victim and abuser live together and a third party (not the victim) has reported the abuse to the police on the victim's behalf.

Based on a review of the literature, the following hypotheses for the study have been identified:

1. There is a significant association between a victim's stated willingness to prosecute and a victim's age: Younger victims will be significantly more likely to state willingness to prosecute their abusers than older victims.

2. There is a significant association between a victim's stated willingness to prosecute and a victim's gender, with female victims being significantly less likely to state willingness to prosecute their abusers than male victims.

3. There is a significant association between victims' race/ethnicity and stated willingness to prosecute, with black victims being more likely to state willingness to prosecute than non-black victims.

4. There is a significant association between a victim's stated willingness to prosecute and an abuser's age: Victims will be significantly more likely to state willingness to prosecute younger abusers than older abusers.

5. There is a significant association between a victim's stated willingness to prosecute and an abuser's gender, with victims being significantly more likely to state willingness to prosecute male abusers than female abusers.

6. There is a significant association between the living arrangements of victims and abusers, and victims' stated willingness to prosecute, with victims who live with their abusers being less likely to state willing to prosecute than those victims who do not live with their abusers.

7. There is a significant association between whether the victim self-reported the abuse to the police or whether an onlooker reported the abuse to the police on the victim's behalf, with the self-reported victim being more likely to state willingness to prosecute the abusers.

8. There is a significant association between the type of abuse experienced by victims and their stated willingness to prosecute, with victims who experience financial abuse being more likely to state willingness to prosecute than victims who experience physical abuse.

9. There is a significant association between the intensity of abuse experienced by victims and their stated willingness to prosecute, with victims who experience low level of abuse being more likely to state willingness to prosecute than those who experience high levels of abuse.

10. Incidents involving victims who state *willingness* to prosecute their abuser offspring are more likely to include the following characteristics: male victim, male abuser, younger victim, younger abuser, be black, experienced financial and low intensity abuse, not live with abuser, and self-reported the abuse to the police.

11. Incidents involving victims who state *unwillingness* to prosecute their abuser offspring are more likely to include the following characteristics: female victim, female abuser, old-old victim, older abuser, be white, experienced physical and high intensity abuse, lives with the abuser, and did not self-report the abuse to the police.

DESCRIPTION OF STUDY POPULATION

The total sample for the study was 295. However, this section's analysis is based on those cases with information on stated willingness to prosecute. As noted in Chapter IV, this reduced the study sample to 238. An analysis of the subset of 238 compared with the total set of 295 complaint reports has confirmed that they are proportionally similar and that therefore the 238 reports are representative of the universe of 295.

DATA ANALYSIS

The first section reports on results of the separate analyses for each of the above research questions. The purpose is to infer which characteristics as described in Chapter IV are significantly associated with victims' stated willingness to prosecute.

Victims' Characteristics Associated with Stated Willingness/Unwillingness to Prosecute their Abusers

The study examined several research questions regarding the relationship between age, gender and ethnicity of the victim and victim's stated willingness to prosecute. As expected, the age of the victim, when categorized as "young-old" (60 to 74 years old) and "old-old" (75 years and above), was found to be associated with stated willingness to prosecute. Younger victims were significantly more likely to state willingness to prosecute their offspring abusers than older victims (see Table 12).

On the other hand, the gender of victims was not found to influence whether or not they would state willingness to prosecute their abusers (see Table 13).

Table 12: Willingness to Prosecute by Age of Victim

Age Category	N	Willing to Prosecute	Unwilling to Prosecute
Age 60-75	195	77%	33%
Age 75+	43	60%	40%

$N = 238$
$(\chi_2 = 4.1, df = 1, p = .042)$

Table 13: Willingness to Prosecute by Gender of Victim

Gender Category	N	Willing to Prosecute	Unwilling to Prosecute
Female	176	74%	26%
Male	62	74%	26%

$N = 238$
$(\chi^2 = .014, df = 1, p = .907)$

Finally, contrary to expectation, race/ethnicity of victims proved to be a significant influence in victims' stated willingness to prosecute their abusers. This was only significant in the case of White and Black victims, however. White elders were significantly less likely to state willingness to prosecute their abusers, while black elders were significantly more likely to state willingness to prosecute their abusers. As may be seen in Table 14, ethnicity was not a significant factor in the decision of Hispanic elders as to whether to state willingness to prosecute their abusers, since they reflect the overall sample proportion of 74%. There was only one Asian victim in the sample of complaint reports, so the Asian category was dropped from the bivariate analysis on the association between willingness to prosecute and race/ethnicity.

(The Asian elder, a female, was a victim of financial abuse by her son, self-reported the abuse, and stated willingness to prosecute her offspring abuser.)

Abuser Characteristics Associated with Victims' Stated Willingness to Prosecute

Additional research questions regarding the relationship between age and gender of the abusers, and the relationship between the victims and abusers, were examined as part of the study. As expected, the age of the abuser influenced victims' stated willingness to prosecute, with victims significantly more likely to state willingness to prosecute younger as opposed to older abusers (see Table 15).

Table 14: Willingness to Prosecute by Ethnicity of Victim

Ethnicity	N	Willing to Prosecute	Unwilling to Prosecute
Black	131	80%	20%
White	49	57%	43%
Hispanic	57	74%	26%

$N = 237$

($x^2 = 9.78$, $df = 2$, $p = .008$)

Table 15: Victims' Willingness to Prosecute by Age of Abuser

Abuser Age Group	N	Willing to Prosecute	Unwilling to Prosecute
Younger (34 years and younger	121	82%	18%
Older (over 34 years)	102	70%	30%

$N = 223$. Complaint reports included 15 with abusers' ages missing.

($x^2 = 3.9$, $df = 1$, $p = .048$)

Also as expected, the gender of the abuser was found to influence victims' decision as to whether to state willingness to prosecute. Victims were significantly more likely to state willingness to prosecute their off-spring abusers when they were male rather than female. Victims were significantly more likely to state willingness to prosecute sons rather than daughters (see Table 16).

Table 16: Victims' Willingness to Prosecute by Gender of Abuser

Abuser Gender	N	Willing to Prosecute	Unwilling to Prosecute
Female	50	56%	44%
Male	188	79%	21%

$N = 238$
$(\chi^2 = 9.4, df = 1, p = .002)$

Structural and Other Characteristics of Sample

As expected, victims who lived with their abusers were found to be significantly less likely to state willingness to prosecute than those who lived apart from their abusers (see Table 17).

However, contrary to expectation, there was no association between self-reporting abuse to the police and victims' stated willingness to prosecute. While proportionately more of the victims who self-reported the abuse to the police also stated willingness to prosecute, the differences were not large enough to be statistically significant (see Table 18).

Table 17: Victims' Stated Willingness to Prosecute by Living Arrangement Between Victim and Abuser

Living Arrangement	N	Willing to Prosecute	Unwilling to Prosecute
Living together	125	69%	31%
Living apart	100	82%	18%
Unknown	13	61%	39%

$N = 238$
$(\chi^2 = 6.12, df = 2, p = .047$

Table 18: Victims' Stated Willingness to Prosecute and Report to Police

(Rep)	N	Willing to Prosecute	Unwilling to Prosecute Reporter
Victim rep	212	75%	25%
Other rep	26	65%	35%

$N = 238$
$(\chi^2 = .669, df = 1, p = .413)$

Categories of criminal offenses, when defined according to types of abuse—physical, financial, and psychological, were not found to be significantly associated with victims' stated willingness to prosecute. There was a tendency for victims of financial abuse to state willingness to prosecute more often than expected, and—conversely—there was a tendency among victims of physical and psychological abuse to state unwillingness to prosecute more frequently than expected. These differences were not sufficient to be statistically significant (see Table 19).

Table 19: Victims' Stated Willingness to Prosecute and Category of Abuse

Abuse Category	N	Willing to Prosecute	Unwilling to Prosecute
Physical	73	69%	31%
Financial	80	81%	19%
Psychological	85	72%	28%

$N = 238$

$(\chi^2 = 3.55, df = 2, p = .169)$

However, when the categories of criminal offenses were defined as high or low intensity abuse, there was a significant association between victims' stated willingness to prosecute and intensity of abuse. Victims experiencing high intensity abuse were significantly more likely to state willingness to prosecute their abusers than those experiencing low level abuse. The findings on structural and other characteristics of the sample as associated with victims' stated willingness to prosecute are presented below (Table 20).

Table 20: Victims' Stated Willingness to Prosecute and Intensity of Abuse

Intensity	N	Willing to Prosecute	Unwilling to Prosecute
High	72	88%	12%
Low	166	68%	30%

$N = 238$

$(\chi^2 = 8.84, df = 1, p = .003)$

OTHER FINDINGS OF INTEREST

Gender-Related Findings

There was no significant association found between the gender of victims and gender of abusers. As noted, the overwhelming majority of victims were female and the abusers were overwhelmingly male (sons). However, taking the differences in proportions of male and female victims and abusers into account, there was no greater likelihood of a male off-spring abusing a female (mother) as opposed to a male (father) victim. This was also the case for female abusers ($\chi^2 = .82$, $df = 1$, $p = .359$).

There was also no significant difference found in the type of abuse perpetrated by the gender of the abuser. However, female abusers were reported as committing more physical abuse and male abusers reported as committing more financial and psychological abuse. These findings are presented in Table 21.

Table 21: Type of Abuse by Gender of Abuser

Abuse Gender	N	Physical	Financial	Psychological
Female	50	40%	26%	34%
Male	188	28%	36%	36%

$N = 238$
($\chi^2 = 2.9$, $df = 2$, $p = .23$)

There was a significant association between intensity of abuse and the victim's gender. Women were significantly more likely to report experiencing low level abuse. Male victims, conversely, were more likely to report high level abuse. These findings are presented in Table 22.

Table 22: Intensity of Abuse by Gender of Victim

Victim	High	Low
Gender	N	Intensity	Intensity
Female	50	25%	75%
Male	188	44%	57%

$N = 238$

$(\chi^2 = 6.19, df = 1, p = .012)$

There was no significant association, however, found between intensity of abuse and the gender of the abuser ($\chi^2 = .22$, $df = 1$, $p = .63$). There was also no significant association between intensity of abuse and the age group of the victims (those 60 to 74 years of age and those 75 years and older ($\chi^2 = .30$, $df = 1$, $p = .58$).

Findings Related to Race/Ethnicity

Examining the relationship between race/ethnicity and type of abuse (categorized as physical, financial, and psychological), there was no significant association among category of abuse and race ethnicity for the sample of 238 ($\chi^2 = 7.72$, $df = 4$, $p = .10$). However, a bivariate analysis utilizing the larger set of 295 complaint reports did show a statistically significant association between category of abuse and race/ethnicity. The significant difference was between Black and White victims, with Black victims significantly more likely to report financial and psychological abuse and White victims significantly more likely to report physical abuse ($\chi^2 = 7.5$, $df = 2$, $p = .023$).

There was a significant association between intensity of abuse and race/ethnicity even using the sample of 238 complaint reports. While the predominant abuse incident reported was of low intensity for all ethnic groups, Black victims were significantly more likely to report experiencing low level as opposed to high level abuse. Both White and Hispanic victims proportionately reported more high level abuse than Blacks. Findings are presented in Table 23.

Table 23: Intensity of Abuse by Race/Ethnicity of Victim

Ethnicity	N	High	Low
Black	131	24%	76%
White	49	35%	65%
Hispanic	57	42%	58%

$N = 237$. The Asian category was dropped for the purpose of this analysis as there was only one reported incident involving an Asian victim. ($x^2 = 6.93$, $df = 2$, $p = .03$

The second part of the data analysis was intended to determine the feasibility of developing a multivariate predictor profile of which elder abuse victims who come to the attention of law enforcement are likely to state willingness to prosecute and which are not. One purpose of the bivariate analysis was to identify those characteristics of elder abuse victims known to NYPD that were and were not significantly associated with stated willingness or unwillingness to prosecute their offspring abusers.

The selection of characteristics hypothesized as likely to form predictor profiles of those elder abuse victims willing and unwilling to prosecute their off-spring abusers was guided by two competing models of elder abuse discussed in the literature involving off-spring: the abuser dependency model (associated with Pillemer) and the caretaker stress model (associated with Steinmetz).

In order to test which, if either, of the predictor profiles (abuser dependency versus caregiver stress) prove most useful in building predictor profiles of elder abuse victims who stated willingness/unwillingness to prosecute their abusers at the time the complaint is filed with the police, a logistic regression was utilized. Included as predictors in the regression were those variables that had been identified as significantly associated with stated willingness to prosecute through the bivariate analyses.

Race/ethnicity was included in the predictor model even though neither Pillemer nor Steinmetz identified race/ethnicity as having predictive value in elder abuse situations. It should be noted, however, that Pillemer and Wolf did include race/ethnicity as part of their description of the subjects studied as part of their four model projects evaluation funded by the Florence Burden Foundation (American Society on Aging, 1991).

In fact, while there is no evidence to suggest that any one racial/ethnic group is more or less prone to domestic violence than any other, some recent studies have emerged suggesting differences in patterns of responses to elder abuse based on race (Black/White). As cited in Chapter II, the United States Department of Justice reported that Blacks report domestic violence to local law enforcement agencies more frequently than other racial/ethnic groups.

In addition, two recent studies (Longres, 1992; Vinton & Williams, 1992) have suggested differences in patterns of abuse among White and Black elderly. As a result, race/ethnicity was included in the regression analysis to determine what variables would contribute to the development of a profile of victims who stated willingness to prosecute their offspring abusers and which did not.

Based on the findings of the bivariate analyses, information on the following variables was not expected to contribute significantly to formulation of a predictor profile of victims' stated willingness/unwillingness to prosecute their abuser offspring:

1.   Gender of victim
2.   Victim reporter to police
3.   Category of abuse (financial/physical/psychological).

The following variables (characteristics) were expected to contribute significantly to the formulation of a predictor profile of elder abuse victims' stated willingness to prosecute their abuser at the time the abuse was first reported to the police:

1.   Age of victim (younger victims will be significantly more likely to state willingness to prosecute than older victims).

2. Age of abuser (victims will be significantly more likely to state willingness to prosecute younger as opposed to older offspring abusers).
3. Gender of abuser (victims will be significantly more likely to state willingness to prosecute male as opposed to female abusers).
4. Race/ethnicity (black victims will be significantly more likely to state willingness to prosecute their offspring abusers than non-blacks).
5. Living arrangement between victim and abuser (victims who do not live with their abusers will be significantly more likely to state willingness to prosecute than those victims who live with their abusers).

In addition to the above, based on the findings of the bivariate analyses—although contrary to the hypothesized profile that low level abuse will be significantly associated with willingness to prosecute and high level abuse significantly associated with stated unwillingness to prosecute—it was anticipated that the following would contribute to a predictor profile of stated willingness to prosecute:

Intensity of abuse (victims experiencing low level abuse will be significantly more likely to state willingness to prosecute their offspring abusers than those experiencing high level abuse).

Multivariate Analysis (Logistic Regression)

To test whether the above variables—identified as significantly associated with stated willingness to prosecute—contributed to the building of a model that predicted which elder abuse victims were likely to state willingness to prosecute an offspring abuser and which were not, a logistic regression was utilized. The results of the logistic regression suggested that when the variables were examined in combination, only four remained significant at the .05 level. These included intensity (type) of abuse ($p = .00$), gender of abuser ($p = .00$), living arrangement between victim and abuser ($p = .03$), and race/ethnicity—black ($p = .04$).

Of the variables that were identified as significant predictors of the outcome, "stated willingness to prosecute," the greatest predictor was intensity of abuse, with high intensity being a strong predictor of "stated willingness to prosecute." Almost equally as powerful was gender of abuser. Other less strong predictors included living arrangement between victim and abuser, and ethnicity when the victim/abuser are black. Findings from the logistic regression are presented in Table 24.

An analysis of the effectiveness of the model developed on the basis of the logistic regression showed that it correctly classified 181 (76%) of the 238 cases and misclassified 57 (24%). For those 176 cases that stated willingness to prosecute, the model correctly classified 163 (93%) and misclassified 13 (7%). For those 62 cases that stated unwillingness to prosecute, the model correctly classified 18 (29%) and misclassified 44 (71%). This means that based on the findings of the logistic regression, the model would have predicted willingness to prosecute in 13 cases when in fact they would have stated unwillingness to prosecute, and unwillingness to prosecute in 44 cases when in fact they would have stated willingness.

Table 24: Logistic Regression Results Predicting Characteristics of Elder Abuse Victims in Relation to Stated Willingness to Prosecute Offspring Abusers

Variable	Coefficient	SD	T-Ratio	Probability
Constant	2.07	1.74	1.20	0.229
Intensity	1.56	0.44	3.51	0.000*
Gender abuser	1.30	0.37	3.50	0.000*
Age abuser	-0.02	0.03	-0.85	0.395
Age victim	-0.02	0.02	-0.90	0.371
Black	0.83	0.42	1.98	0.047*
White	-0.44	0.48	-0.92	0.356
Living arrangement	-0.77	0.36	-2.16	0.031*
Log of likelihood function	-114.698562			
Chi-square statistic for significance of equation	43.698562			
Degrees of freedom for chi-square statistic	7			
Significance level for chi-square statistic	0.0000			

*Significant at the < .05 level

This suggests that the model is better at predicting stated willingness to prosecute than stated unwillingness to prosecute. The chi-square level of significance for the logistic regression was .00, suggesting that these findings could not have occurred by chance alone. The findings are presented in Table 25.

Table 25: Observed Incidents Correctly Classified by Model According to Whether Victim Stated Willingness/Unwillingness to Prosecute Offspring Abusers

	Willing		Unwilling		Total	
Correct	163	(93%)	18	(29%)	181	(76%)
Incorrect	13	(7%)	44	(71%)	57	(24%)
Total	207	(100%)	31	(100%)	238	(100%)

It should be noted that by predicting that every case would state willingness to prosecute, it would be also possible to predict correctly in 74% of the cases for the study population, as 74%—in fact—did state willingness to prosecute. Using the predictor model developed through the logistic regression, it may be possible to more effectively predict stated willingness/ unwillingness to prosecute with subsequent populations, however.

CLASSIFICATION AND REGRESSION TREES (CART)

To further verify the predictive value of the variables on the police complaint report in relation to a victim's stated willingness to prosecute the offspring abuser, it was decided to utilize another method of multivariate analysis. As a result, a Classification and Regression Tree (CART) analysis was also performed. CART is a single procedure that can be used to analyze either categorical (classification) or continuous data (regression). According to the SYSTAT (1992) manual: "A defining feature of CART is that it presents its results in the form of decision trees. . . CART is inherently a non- parametric methodology that communicates by pictures" (p. 11).

Utilizing the CART methodology, the association between stated willingness to prosecute and the identified predictor variables were further clarified. The most significant predictor of stated willingness/unwillingness to prosecute was intensity of abuse. Of those victims who experienced high intensity abuse, 63 (88%) out of 72 stated willingness to prosecute. This emerged as the single predictor of stated willingness to prosecute for those victims who experienced high intensity abuse, supporting the findings of the logistic regression. It was the most important predictor regardless of gender, living situation and race/ethnicity.

Of those who experienced low intensity abuse, Blacks showed a greater likelihood of prosecuting than non-Blacks—77 (77%) out of 100 Blacks who experienced low intensity abuse stated willingness to prosecute, as opposed to 36 (55%) out of 66 non-Blacks). For those Blacks who experienced low intensity abuse, however, the gender of the abuser was the most significant predictor of stated willingness to prosecute: Black elders who experienced low intensity abuse from female offspring were as likely to state willingness to prosecute as not: Eleven (50%) stated willingness compared with 11 (50%) stated unwillingness to prosecute. When male offspring committed the low level abuse, however, Black elders were significantly more likely to state willingness to prosecute than not—66 (85%) stated willingness to prosecute and 12 (15%) stated unwillingness to prosecute.

This suggests that intensity of abuse, race/ethnicity, and gender of the abuser have important interactive effects in relation to stated willingness to prosecute. Each of these variables has different effects on the dependent variable, depending on its status with respect to the other two. For example, severity of abuse is predictive of stated willingness to prosecute by the victim, but how predictive it is depends on race (of both victim and abuser in the case of off-spring abuse) and gender of the abuser.

The CART analysis further demonstrates that living arrangements between victims and abusers is not a significant predictor variable either, as suggested by the logistic regression. Once race, gender of abuser, and severity of abuse are accounted for, the predictive value of living arrangements between victims and abusers becomes insignificant.

Of the variables examined as potential predictor variables of an elder abuse victim's stated willingness/unwillingness to prosecute, the CART analysis identified high intensity abuse as the key predictor variable. This suggests that by knowing a victim experienced high intensity abuse, one can predict with a strong degree of certainty—according to this model—that he or she will state willingness to prosecute his or her offspring abuser—regardless of age, ethnicity, living arrangement with abuser, or whether the victim self-reported the abuse to the police.

A second key predictor of stated willingness to prosecute based on the CART analysis—when the victim has experienced low level abuse—is race/ethnicity (the victim is Black). A third predictor, which has an interactive effect with race/ethnicity, is the gender of the abuser (the abuser is a Black male offspring).

The "tree" diagram illustrates the interrelationship among these predictor variables as identified by the CART analysis. This program "prunes" the tree at the point the variables cease having significant predictive value: Hence, none of the other variables examined in the study appear as part of the tree. CART clarifies the logistic regression in that Black victims where the abuser is male are likely to state willingness to prosecute even when the abuse is of low intensity. The results of the CART analysis are presented in Table 26.

Second Logistic Regression

The CART analysis, unlike the logistic regression, did not identify "living arrangement between victim and abuser" as a significant predictor of victims' stated willingness to prosecute. Based on the results of the CART analysis, a second logistic regression was run, using only the variables "severity of abuse," "gender of abuser," and "Black race/ethnicity" as predictor variables in the logistic equation. The purpose was to determine the impact of dropping this variable from the logistic regression on the model's ability to correctly classify incidents according to whether the victims stated willingness or unwillingness to prosecute their offspring abusers.

Table 26: CART Analysis of Predictor Variables of Stated Willingness/Unwillingness to Prosecute Offspring Abusers by Elder Abuse Victims

Low Intensity Abuse	High Intensity Abuse
53-	9-
113+	63+
$\underline{p}$ = .67	$\underline{p}$ = .88
Non-Black Victim	Black Victim
30-	23-
36+	77+
$\underline{p}$ = .55	$\underline{p}$ = .77
Female Abuser	Male Abuser
11-	12-
11+	66+
$\underline{p}$ = .5	$\underline{p}$ = .85

<u>Note.</u>   +: Will prosecute
-: Will not prosecute
p: Proportion prosecuting

In this second logistic regression, 179 (75%) cases were classified correctly and 59 (25%) were misclassified. This was slightly less accurate than the first logistic regression: In the second regression, four (2%) fewer cases were classified correctly. Because less information was needed for the second model to make an equivalent prediction, however, the second model appears to be more useful in quick decision making without a significant increase in error. Thus, collecting data on these items alone would be helpful to police in deciding how to proceed with follow-up to reports reflecting elder abuse.

DISCUSSION

A number of the variables reflected in police complaint reports were significantly associated with stated willingness to prosecute, as demonstrated by the results of the bivariate analyses. However, multivariate analytic techniques showed that a smaller group of these variables were found to predict stated willingness to prosecute as efficiently in the study population.

The variable with strongest predictive value was intensity of abuse: This emerged as the single most powerful predictor of stated willingness to prosecute—cutting across gender of victim and abuser, age of victim and abuser, living arrangement between victim and abuser, race/ethnicity, and type of abuse. Age of victim and abuser were identified through bivariate analyses as being significantly associated with willingness on the part of the victim to prosecute, but these variables showed high colinearity, and disappeared as key predictors of stated willingness to prosecute in the logistic and CART regressions.

A subsample of abuse victims in the study also demonstrated stated willingness to prosecute in instances of low intensity abuse. These included Black victims who were abused by male offspring. These factors were not significant for non-Black (White and Hispanic elderly victims) included in the study.

The hypothesis was not substantiated that a predictor profile of elder victims of offspring abuse who state willingness to prosecute to police at the time of the abuse complaint could be identified that included gender of victim and abuser, age of victim and abuser, living arrangements between victim and abuser, race/ethnicity of victim/abuser and self-reporting to the police. High intensity abuse experienced by an elderly victim of domestic violence by offspring was the single predictor of victims' stating willingness to prosecute the abuser at the time of the police report regardless of other factors.

Gender of abuser and race/ethnicity of victim/offspring abuser together were predictive of a victim's stated willingness to prosecute when experiencing low level abuse: Black victims were identified as likely to state willingness to prosecute their offspring abuser when the abuser was a son. Abuser gender and race/ethnicity did not have predictive value under circumstances of low level abuse when the victim was non-Black.

Neither the hypothesized abuser dependency model of elder abuser associated with Pillemer nor the caregiver stress model of elder abuse associated with Steinmetz appeared to have predictive value (for the purposes of the study) in determining when an elder abuse victim would state willingness or unwillingness to prosecute his/her offspring abuser. Race/ethnicity was never considered a key predictor of elder abuse by Pillemer or his associates. Intensity of abuse was a concern to researchers like Steinmetz who focused on caregiver stress, but much concern centered on the victim's inability to protect or advocate on behalf of him or herself when exposed to severe abuse, for fear of losing whatever familial support was available. As noted, the findings indicate that older victims of domestic mistreatment state willingness to prosecute high intensity abuse regardless of other factors examined in the study.

Only the finding that victims would be more likely to state willingness to prosecute male abusers was not surprising, based on findings from the literature to date that older people depend on daughters more than sons for caregiving and other affective support. However, the finding that victims stated willingness to prosecute female offspring abusers proportional to what may be expected suggests factors other than those reflected on police complaint reports and examined in the present study influence the decisions of older victims of domestic violence to prosecute their offspring abusers.

Two-Way Analysis of Variance (ANOVA)

Neither the logistic regression or the CART defined ages of victims and abusers as significant predictors of victims' stated willingness/unwillingness to prosecute their off-spring abuser. This is in spite of the results of the tests of association that indicated significant associations between ages of victims and abusers and victims' stated willingness to prosecute.

In order to further examine the relationship between ages of victims and abusers and victims' stated willingness to prosecute, a two-way ANOVA was utilized to look for interaction effects among ages of victims and abusers and victims' stated willingness to prosecute. The results of the ANOVA showed that the ages of victims were related to ethnicity but not to stated willingness to prosecute their abusers. White victims were the oldest, with a mean age of 72 years; Black victims were the next oldest, with a mean age of 69; and Hispanic victims were the youngest as a group, with a mean age of 67. Differences between mean ages of White and Black victims were significant at the .009 level, and differences between Whites and Hispanics were significant at the .000 level. However, differences between Black and Hispanic victims were not statistically significant. The ANOVA further demonstrated that there was no relationship between victims' age and ethnicity as a group ($p = .17$) and there was no significant interaction effect among victims' age, ethnicity, and stated willingness to prosecute
($p = .82$).

The results of the ANOVA demonstrated that for the abusers, age was related to ethnicity for all three ethnic groups in the study. The oldest abusers were White, with a mean age of 38; the mean age for Black abusers was 35, and—for Hispanics—the mean age was 29. The difference between mean ages of White and Black abusers was significant at the .016 level; the difference between mean ages of White and Hispanic abusers was significant at the .000 level, and the difference between Black and Hispanic abusers was significant at the .000 level. In addition, victims were significantly more likely to state willingness to prosecute younger abusers ($p = .047$); however, this difference was confined to White and Black abusers (p = .008).

Overall, these differences disappeared once the interaction effect among age of abuser, ethnicity of abuser and victims' stated willingness to prosecute was taken into account (p = .92.) In conclusion, the ANOVA validates the findings of the logistic regression and the CART that the ages of abusers and victims are not significant predictors of which elder abuse victims are and are not likely to state willingness to prosecute their off-spring abuser at the time the initial complaint is filed.

CHAPTER VI

Conclusion

The study on elder abuse and law enforcement in New York City (Manhattan) intended to achieve the following objectives:

1. Describe a profile of elderly victims of domestic mistreatment by offspring. The study sample is drawn from elderly Manhattan residents who came to the attention of the New York City Police Department (NYPD) in 1992.
2. Expand the knowledge base of criminal offenses reported to the NYPD in Manhattan that are reflective of elder abuse as defined in the elder abuse literature.
3. Test the feasibility of developing predictor profiles of elder abuse victims who state willingness/unwillingness to prosecute their offspring abusers at the time the abuse incident is first reported to the police.
4. Identify policy proposals for law enforcement, implications for social work, limitations and needed follow-up based on findings of the study.

DESCRIPTION OF ELDER ABUSE AS REPORTED TO THE NYPD IN MANHATTAN IN 1992

The average age of elder abuse victims in the sample fell into the young-old category (the mean age was 69). The oldest reported victim was 93 years of age, but this reflected an outlier. The oldest abuse victims on average were found to be White, with the next oldest Black and the youngest Hispanic victims; however, the average ages of Black and White victims were not significantly different. This pattern also held true for abusers, as could be expected with offspring abuse, except that significant age differences emerged among all three ethnic groups for abusers: White abusers were—on average—the oldest, Black abusers were significantly younger than White abusers, and Hispanic abusers were younger as a group than both White and Black abusers.

For those victims stating willingness to prosecute, younger victims on average demonstrated greater willingness to prosecute their abusers than older victims. However, an analysis of patterns within ethnic groups showed that in interaction with race/ethnicity, this association disappeared and victims' age was not found to be a key predictor variable of willingness to prosecute. It was likely an artifact of the way victims were grouped into "young-old" and "old-old" categories for the purpose of performing the bivariate analyses.

The gender of victims was overwhelmingly female (mothers)—74%—and that of abusers overwhelmingly male (sons). While Pillemer has challenged the notion that gender of victim was a key defining variable (Pillemer & Finkelhor, 1988), there is otherwise general agreement in the elder abuse literature that women are the predominant victims of elder mistreatment (Carlson, 1992).

Carlson identifies this as primarily due to the fact that women represent the majority of elderly people today. A comparison with the ratio of older women to men in Manhattan and New York City as a whole showed that it was not statistically different from that of the study population (at the .07 level of significance). Carlson also states that studies show daughters are the primary perpetrators of elder abuse: This was not reflected in the findings of this study. The overwhelming proportion of abusers were males (sons).

The tendency of Black elders to report even low levels of abuse with greater frequency than other ethnic groups supports the findings of national studies that Blacks utilize the criminal justice system to report domestic violence with greater frequency than other ethnic groups. This may be reflective of the lower income levels (on average) among Blacks, which may be prompting this group to seek redress from local law enforcement not as an agent of social control, but as a provider of social services or in lieu of more expensive legal services. On the other hand, Hispanic elders have an even lower average income level in New York City (Cantor, 1993), and do not report abuse to the police at the same rate as older Blacks. This suggests that further research is needed to determine the reasons for high reporting by Blacks elders, relative to their proportion within the population.

Race/ethnicity differentiates on other demographic variables as well. (It should be noted that race is used in the study as a surrogate value for culture in the anthropological sense and not as a genetic indicator.) Age differences for both victims and abusers are striking between ethnic groups. While not a major focus of the study, Hispanic victims and abusers were significantly younger, on average, than either Blacks or Whites.

Physical abuse appeared more predominant among White victims/abusers, and financial and psychological abuse appeared more predominant among Black victims/abusers. While expected, this was not statistically significant in the sample of 238; however, it was statistically significant in the analysis of the larger set of 295 complaint reports. This could suggest some support for the hypothesis by Vinton and Williams (1992) that social isolation may make White victims more susceptible to physical abuse and the combination of extended families and economic discrimination against younger Blacks may increase the risk of financial abuse among Black elders. There was no pattern among Hispanic elders as to a predominant type of abuse experienced.

In a recent study of older people in New York City in the 1990s, children of African-American respondents were the most likely (17%) to be living in the same household as their older parents, followed by Latino children (13%) and, finally, (8%) White children (Cantor, 1993). There were insufficient data available on study subjects through the NYPD complaint reports to identify a link between reported elder abuse and family composition, however.

While males were by far the most predominant perpetrators of reported abuse, the primary types of abuse reported as committed by them were financial and psychological. Female abusers were more likely to be reported for committing physical abuse.

Slightly more elders in the study lived with, as opposed to apart from, their abusers; however, there was close to a 50-50 split. Elders living with their abusers were less likely to state willingness to prosecute their offspring abusers than those who did not live with the abuser. This factor, however, did not emerge as a significant predictor of willingness to prosecute in the multivariate (CART) analysis.

The fact that most elders, regardless of whether they lived with their abusers or not, reported the abuse to the police themselves suggests a degree of self-reliance that would not have been anticipated from the caregiver stress/frail and impaired victim model. This could reflect a limitation of the study, however. Impaired victims may be less likely to show up in a sample drawn from police complaint reports (as opposed to adult protective services caseloads, for example).

The willingness to report abuse to the police on the part of elders in the study was striking. In addition, the preponderance of low level abuse reported may mean that elders are willing to report abuse in the initial stages of the abuse cycle. (Findings of studies on spouse abuse have suggested that abuse tends to escalate over time.)

The strong predictive value of severity of abuse to stated willingness to prosecute may also be reflective of the fact that the abuse has escalated over time. While the study did not examine the possibility of multiple complaint reports made by complainants in the study, this may have in fact have been the case in some instances. Thus, at the time of the report of severe abuse, the elder may have reached a threshold of tolerance of the abuse and be most likely to be willing to prosecute. There may also be increased concern on the part of the elders stating willingness to prosecute in the face of severe abuse, reflecting a felt need for protection.

CRIMINAL OFFENSES REPORTED TO NYPD REFLECTIVE OF ELDER ABUSE

Unlike most studies of agency reports of elder abuse, the types of abuse reflected in the study are almost equally divided among physical, psychological and financial abuse (utilizing the coding scheme of counting one type of abuse per incidence report, based on a hierarchy of abuse categories: first physical, then financial, and finally, psychological). Financial abuse in particular is considered an important form of elder abuse (Abelman, 1992). It had been overlooked as a form of domestic violence by the NYPD, however, which has to date identified only those offenses reflective of domestic violence most likely to apply across the life span (physical and psychological).

Financial abuse is one category of abuse that is particularly characteristic of elder abuse, as opposed to child or spouse abuse. This could be an indirect effect of social policies that since the passage of the Social Security Act of 1935 have increasingly raised elders to or above the poverty level and guaranteed a monthly income (however meager) through Social Security, Supplemental Security Income (SSI), and pensions.

Elder abuse victims in the study were subjected to a wide variety of criminal offenses by offspring. These ranged from harassment (including stalking), menacing, assault, robbery, forgery, and even rape. The litany of criminal offenses by offspring read no differently than those committed by strangers against the elderly. However, while elders can take measures to protect themselves against stranger crime by refusing to admit strangers into their homes, avoiding leaving their homes in the evenings, seeking well-protected outdoor environments, and maintaining well-secured residences, these measures often offer limited protection against off-spring abusers.

Some of the descriptions of abuse reported by elderly victims to the police offer poignant examples of criminal offenses committed against them by offspring: the mother who invites her son for dinner and finds—when her back is turned—he leaves without saying goodbye, taking her radio with him; the father who opens the door to his son to be hit on the head and threatened with a box cutter; the grandparent who arranges a visit between his daughter and her child for whom he is caring—with the result that she steals a gold chain off the grandchild's neck and disappears. The fact the elders reported these incidents to the police could be seen as a measure of the hurt, anger, and sense of rejection experienced.

In spite of the poignancy and—in some instances—horror evoked by the reports of abuse as described in the police complaint reports, the elderly victims making the reports emerge as a spunky group who are willing to take steps to protest the abuse by offspring. This shows that a significant number of elder abuse victims are willing to report abuse to the police on their own, or cooperate once the report is made by a third party witness.

Advocates of mandatory reporting for elder abuse suggest otherwise: that elderly victims of domestic violence by offspring will not report abuse to the police—much less state willingness to prosecute their abuser. While the findings of the study appear to challenge this, it is not possible—given the scope of the study—to determine if there were many more victims who did not report.

At least for the group of Manhattan elders who self-reported complaints against offspring abuse with the NYPD, the position appears to be supported that elder victims of abuse are not only capable of advocating on their own behalf, but view the police as a valuable resource and as allies in ensuring protection from abuse. The candor with which some of the victims in the study shared intimate and potentially embarrassing details of the abuse to the responding police officer suggests a level of comfort on the part of the elderly victim in speaking to the officer. This in turn supports findings from the literature on the trust older people feel toward police (Yin, 1985). It also suggests that local law enforcement can play a valuable role within communities in identifying and responding to elder abuse.

FEASIBILITY OF DEVELOPING PREDICTOR PROFILES OF ELDER ABUSE VICTIMS' WILLINGNESS/ UNWILLINGNESS TO PROSECUTE THEIR ABUSERS

Neither the hypothesized abuser dependency model of elder abuser associated with Pillemer nor the caregiver stress model of elder abuse associated with Steinmetz (for the purposes of the study) appeared to have predictive value in determining when an elder abuse victim would state willingness or unwillingness to prosecute his/her offspring abuser. Race/ethnicity was not considered a key predictor of elder abuse by Pillemer or his associates. Intensity of abuse was a concern to researchers like Steinmetz, who focused on caregiver stress, but much concern centered on the victim's inability to protect or advocate on behalf of him or herself from severe abuse, for fear of losing whatever familial support was available. As noted, the findings indicate that older victims of domestic mistreatment who report such abuse state willingness to prosecute high intensity abuse regardless of other factors examined in the study.

To summarize, the profile of abuse-reporting victims stating willingness to prosecute emerged that included those who experienced high intensity abuse (irrespective of age, gender, ethnicity, relationship to or living arrangement with the abuser and who reported the abuse to the police), and Black victims of low level abuse when the abuser was a son. Less likely to state willingness to prosecute were White or Hispanic abuse-reporting victims who experienced low level abuse and Black victims reporting low level abuse by daughters.

IMPLICATIONS OF DEVELOPING PREDICTOR PROFILES OF ELDER ABUSE VICTIMS' WILLINGNESS/ UNWILLINGNESS TO PROSECUTE THEIR ABUSERS

As noted in Chapter I, implications for service intervention follow from clients' assessed likelihood of stating willingness or unwillingness to prosecute their offspring abusers. Teamwork between precinct-based police and community-based social workers is essential to ensure appropriate intervention strategies.

Elder abuse victims who are assessed as likely to state willingness to prosecute could be encouraged to report the abusive incident to the police and, in addition, counseled and supported through the process of follow-up. This may involve application to the family or criminal courts for orders of protection and instructions on their use. It may also involve working with clients as they engage the District Attorney's office. For clients who are reluctant to pursue prosecution with the District Attorney's office if it means incarceration of a loved one who is abusing them, District Attorneys' offices in New York City are expanding options for alternative to incarceration (ATI) sentences to include mandated counseling, substance abuse treatment, or evaluation by mental health professionals. Assisting victims to view prosecution as a means of obtaining help for offspring abusers can ease the guilt elder abuse victims may feel while ensuring protection from further abuse.

For clients assessed as unlikely to state willingness to prosecute, encouraging and assisting them to file a complaint report with the local precinct anyway can still be useful. It can demonstrate to the elder abuse victim that the police can be useful as a resource, and still allow them to maintain control over the outcome of the complaint process, if they are not ready to move more assertively against their off-spring abusers. Additional protective services can be discussed with those victims assessed as unlikely to prosecute and incorporated into a service plan. For non-judgment impaired victims, these may include occasional visits by the community police, new locks for the doors, home visits or regular telephone contacts by social service professionals, aides, or volunteers, meals on wheels, voluntary money management, and instructions on how to contact the police in the case of an emergency. For judgment-impaired victims or those who appear be in imminent danger, more aggressive interventions such as referrals to adult protective services may be indicated. This can also apply to mentally impaired abusers of unimpaired elder abuse victims, as well. As noted, coordinated efforts between police and social workers to assist elder abuse victims and their families are often the key to success in ensuring victims' safety and protection.

POLICY IMPLICATIONS

Implications for the NYPD

While broader implications may be drawn, within the context of the system in which the study was carried out, the study's findings demonstrated that at least for some elder abuse victims, the police are seen as an important resource in their seeking protection against victimization by offspring. To date, no state has specifically legislated mandatory reporting to the local police department. Indiana mandates reporting of elder abuse to county District Attorney offices; however, reports are received and investigated by outstationed APS workers, according to Dr. Ronald Dolan, Professor, Ball State University School of Social Work in Indiana (telephone conversation, October 1993). The Charleston, South Carolina, Police Department, however, has developed a unique program that includes a 24-hour hotline for reporting elder abuse: South Carolina has a mandatory reporting system (Charleston Police Department, Undated Brochure). Most states with mandatory or voluntary reporting systems designate local or state area aging agencies or adult protective service agencies to receive and follow up on reports of elder abuse.

For states like New York that do not have a mandatory reporting system, reports of abuse may come to the attention of the local area aging agency, adult protective services agency, local voluntary agency, or the police. Of the available options, the police department is rarely considered an important source of reporting and follow-up for elder abuse. In addition, the problems in getting information on elder abuse reports from police departments make them difficult to use for social service purposes.

In spite of these limitations, however, NYPD has taken significant steps to ensure responsiveness to reports of domestic violence. Training is mandated on procedures to be used in instances of child and spouse abuse. Victim Services Agency (VSA) has a long-standing relationship with both NYPD and the New York City Housing Authority police; a demonstration project was undertaken in 12 precincts citywide where a VSA worker was co-located at a precinct to follow up on complaint reports involving domestic violence. The Protective Services for Adults (PSA) Agency within the Human Resources Administration (the social services arm of the New York City municipal government) works with NYPD on cases that have been identified as involving criminal mistreatment or exploitation of older people. The Mayor's Office expanded the "Safe Streets, Safe City" campaign to include "Safe Homes" as well; the NYC Department for the Aging (DFTA) was identified as the lead mayoral agency for this initiative as it applied to elder abuse. Some community based agencies—notably Manhattan's West Side One Stop for Senior Services—have developed exemplary service program components for abused and exploited elders in their catchment areas using demonstration grant funding.

Continuing budget shortfalls on both local and state levels of government threaten the expansion of all these initiatives to address elder abuse as a domestic violence issue of concern. To ensure the continuation of efforts to address elder abuse through the criminal justice system, a number of steps could be taken by NYPD. These include:

1. Strengthening the Community Policing Program to make it an effective precinct-based link between victims of social problems like elder abuse and the agencies that can effectively service them.

2. Modifying police training curricula to ensure that police responding on crimes reflecting elder abuse know to identify them as such to improve front-line case detection. Financial abuse by family members, when reported by elders to police, should be identified as a form of domestic violence. In addition, training on the "syndrome" of domestic violence, including elder abuse, that constrains some victims from agreeing to prosecute should be provided to counter possible frustration by police who respond to elder abuse complaints.

3. Institutionalizing the use of supplementary reporting forms for police that incorporate information on formal and informal supports available/utilized by elders reporting abuse by family members, for more effective follow-up to complaints.

4. Expanding NYPD crime prevention programs to include public education and information on the detection and prevention of elder abuse.

5. Encouraging more collaboration on a community level between community based agencies serving the elderly and the local precincts to effectively address the problem of elder abuse in the community.

6. Considering the addition of civilians such as forensic social workers in the NYPD workforce.

Community-based public education initiatives—part of the Community Policing Program mandate—should stress that elder mistreatment by family members is not only a domestic violence problem, but may reflect criminal acts that could result in arrest and prosecution of the abuser. It should also stress that elder abuse is not necessarily synonymous with criminal acts, and that support for overwhelmed caregivers is available in communities and should be utilized before family problems involving an older adult escalate out of control.

The community policing effort in New York City offers an excellent opportunity for collaboration with community-based service agencies. However, collaborative relationships will have limited success as long as confidentiality mandates on the part of the police preclude sharing client-specific information on complaint reports representing elder abuse situations. Aggressive pursuit of ways to circumvent these restrictions by both local law enforcement and community-based and public social service agencies could result in improved quality of life and safety of elderly community residents who are victims of family violence and exploitation.

Forensic social workers based in precincts who can supervise social work student units and/or community liaisons could prove a vital adjunct to police on the beat and the Community Policing Program in evaluating the service needs of elder abuse victims. They can also ensure appropriate referrals to HRA's Protective Services for Adults, the DFTA-funded community-based aging network, and VSA's neighborhood-based crime victims program sites. A study of elder abuse and adult protective services in New York City found that only 4% of referrals came from law enforcement (Abelman, 1992). While this could be a reflection of a need for additional training to sensitize police to the problem of elder abuse and the need for appropriate follow-up, police would rarely have the expertise to make the kind of sophisticated clinical assessments sometimes needed to identify an elderly victim of family abuse who lacks capacity for self-determination.

One collaborative model between police and social workers that shows promise is utilized by New York City Housing Authority (NYCHA) police and social service staff. Complaint reports representing elder abuse in New York City public housing projects are routinely given to NYCHA social service staff to follow up on. In these situations, confidentiality issues are not relevant as police and social work staff are all part of the same agency (NYCHA). The decision by New York City to combine NYPD, Transit, and NYCHA police into one administrative unit may ultimately provide an opportunity for extending this policy to local precincts. Another proven model, as noted, is outstationing voluntary sector social service workers at local precincts: VSA has demonstrated the effectiveness of this as an alternative to the use of civilian social work staff in the NYPD. Currently, funding constraints could threaten the expansion of this noteworthy program.

Implications for Social Work Practice

The police are trained as agents of public safety and control; they are not trained social workers. Domestic violence in general and elder abuse in particular are reflective of complex family dynamics that often require the evaluation and intervention skills of trained social work professionals.

Stated unwillingness to prosecute could be reflective of a competent older adult's assessment that the present situation does not represent sufficient danger to his or her safety as to escalate beyond the initial incident reported to the police. On the other hand, it may reflect an older person's fear of retribution by the abuser, or a felt sense of loyalty, or need to protect the offspring abuser that overrides the older person's survival instincts. For an impaired elder, it could be reflective of a fear of abandonment or withdrawal of even minimal caregiving support, or of judgment that is sufficiently impaired as to render the victim incapable of accurately assessing the extent of danger they may be facing from the abuser.

In addition, elder abuse victims, like domestic violence victims in general, are often reluctant to report or press charges against their abusers when they are family members. Social workers who come in contact with such victims, particularly if the abuse is long-term, on-going, and chronic, may choose to use persistence as well as patience as part of their intervention strategy. This has been identified as a strategy of "negotiated consent," as opposed to passive acceptance of a client's right to self-determination, if the client is judged to be in danger or at risk of further abuse (Moody, personal communication, 1990).

For older victims of domestic mistreatment, stating willingness to prosecute on the part of elderly victims does not guarantee follow-through with prosecution or obtaining an order of protection in spite of the possible dangers with which the victims may be faced. This study did not track cases through the criminal justice system, but only reviewed them at the initial point of contact with the police. However, ongoing assistance may be necessary to assist those victims who state willingness to prosecute their abusers negotiate the criminal justice or court process to obtain needed protection. Monitoring and/or assistance with food, money management, personal care, repairing of locks, and securing of windows may be necessary—all services local social service agencies for the elderly can provide if linked to the victim at the time of the report or shortly thereafter.

One of the stumbling blocks in intervening in elder abuse cases is the attachment the abuse victim often feels for the offspring abuser, in spite of the abuse experienced. A vivid example of this can be seen in Spike Lee's movie, *Jungle Fever*, in which the actress Ruby Dee portrays a mother victimized by a beloved son who is a crack addict. Unlike stranger crime, elder abuse by offspring involves family members who may have strong emotional ties. As a result, it may be essential to address the problems and needs of the abuser in order to ensure the protection and safety of the victim.

For social workers, the value of differentiating among clients who report abuse by offspring, or who are assessed as being at risk of abuse, in relation to their assessed likelihood of stating willingness to prosecute their offspring abusers is that more effective targeting of interventions can be accomplished. For the family dispute cases, family mediation counseling as advocated by Gelles (Mancuso, 1989) may be most effective. For those victims who are predicted to be unlikely to state willingness to prosecute, evaluation for adult protective services could be indicated. If an APS referral is not deemed to be appropriate, keeping in touch with the victim by phone or through the assistance of building superintendents or bank personnel could serve as a measure of protection, particularly if the victimization continues and the victim at a later point becomes ready to take action against it.

As noted, victims who are predicted to be likely to state willingness to prosecute may need assistance in following through with the process of cooperating with the district attorney's office and/or negotiating the court system to obtain an order of protection. In addition, the elderly victim's environment should be investigated to ensure that it is made as secure as possible. The family network could be evaluated to determine if other family members could offer protection and/or support for the elderly victim against further abuse by the offspring abuser. Finally, the abuser should be evaluated—if possible—to determine if problems that led to committing the abusive act could be addressed through social service interventions or substance abuse or mental health services.

Three major intervention models identified by Wolf (1990) include Statutory or Mandatory Reporting (most often associated with child abuse); the Legal Intervention Model, which reflects a criminal justice approach, and the Advocacy or Social Service Intervention Model, which could include an empowerment approach (associated with spouse abuse) or a protective services approach, when the adult victim appears to be incapable of protecting him or herself against the abuse or exploitation. Several social service intervention models that show promise for assisting both competent and judgement impaired elder abuse victims have been developed by social workers (for example, Breckman, with Adelman—a physician, and Tomita, with Quinn—a nurse and court investigator) (Breckman & Adelman, 1988; Quinn & Tomita, 1997; 1986). These models have not been subject to rigorous evaluation as to effectiveness to date (U.S. House of Representatives, 1990).

Financial abuse of elderly victims in inner-city communities—particularly within the Black communities—could be reflective of larger social issues such as unusually high unemployment among inner-city Black males, poor or non-existent housing resources, easy availability of crack-cocaine and prevalence of violence on the streets. Social policies intended to stimulate economic development, employment programs targeted to inner-city minority communities, stricter gun controls, greater availability of substance abuse treatment and detoxification programs, increased resources for housing and environmental improvements, community-based access to social services and other strategies for improving living conditions in inner cities for family members of all ages could serve to address some of the abuse experienced by Black (as well as Hispanic) elders. The social work profession has a long history of advocating on behalf of social welfare programs for the poor and disadvantaged, and social work practice should also include continued efforts in this direction.

Resources are increasingly being allocated for criminal justice as they are being withdrawn from the social services community. This suggests that social work as a profession needs to begin to look at how it can work within the criminal justice system to address issues of domestic violence. The findings of this study suggest that such social services programs for the elderly located within the criminal justice system would prove valuable. This in turn could provide an opportunity for schools of social work and the NYPD to establish a social work presence through student units supervised by field instructors on the staff of NYPD or outstationed from social services agencies as a means of developing social work components in local precincts, to enhance the community policing effort.

Social workers based at precincts permit timely follow-up on complaints representing elder abuse as an effective way of assisting older victims of domestic mistreatment. Assessments undertaken by precinct-based forensic social workers on elderly complainants of abuse by offspring can result in successful interventions targeted to the needs of the individual victim/clients.

Forensic social work is a field of practice that is getting increased attention from the profession (Ivanoff, Smyth, & Finnegan, 1993). While to date it has been seen as a component of correctional services within prison facilities, there is a movement toward community based forensic social work: A social work student unit has been established effective 1993 in the Mid-Town Manhattan Community Court, a demonstration project funded by the City of New York, the New York State Office of Court Administration (OCA), local business and community groups, the New York Community Trust, and the Rockefeller Foundation (among other funding sources) and administered by the Fund for the City of New York as an important experiment in community-based court administration for misdemeanor-level crimes.

Hiring social workers at local precincts to work with community police and support police responding to domestic violence situations—particularly those involving the elderly—could provide a valuable service to the police and victims alike. In addition, this could provide the needed bridge between social work practice and the criminal justice system in responding to the needs of elder abuse victims living in the community. Social workers hired for this purpose may require special orientation and training to work effectively within a law enforcement setting.

Forensic social work, as defined by the Legal Aid Society, involves working within the criminal justice system to interview clients, diagnose, evaluate and develop a service plan in conjunction with criminal justice personnel, work with the District Attorney's office in developing alternative sentencing plans, court advocacy, make referrals, and provide crisis intervention counseling. Forensic social workers can also serve as field instructors for units of social work students (as in the Manhattan Midtown Community Court Model) and/or supervise teams of community liaisons who network with community-based programs and other agencies (including family and criminal courts when orders of protection are needed), make home visits, and assist in developing and following up on service plans for linking victims—and their abusers as appropriate—with government entitlements, as well as community-based social, health and mental health programs (Legal Aid Society, 1993).

Schools of social work could consider adding some elective courses on social work within the criminal justice system. This may not only include an orientation to the criminal justice system and the state penal code, but to issues of mutual concern to the fields of social work and law enforcement—such as domestic violence and victims' services, as well as treatment and transitional services for the forensic mentally ill and other impaired populations who increasingly come to the attention of the criminal justice system: substance abusers, people with AIDS and tuberculosis, the physically impaired and developmentally disabled, and—increasingly—pregnant, parenting, and post-partum women.

The special concerns of older adults who are victimized by family members should be addressed within the context of an understanding of gerontology and families in later life. The course work could not only focus on clinical issues, but policy and planning issues as well, to begin to develop leadership capacity within the social work community in shaping the response of the criminal justice system to domestic violence victims and their families as well as other special populations. A systems approach, such as that used by the Fordham University Graduate School of Social Service, is well suited as a conceptual framework for understanding the relationships among individuals, family systems, community service systems, the criminal justice system, and the social welfare system.

LIMITATIONS OF STUDY AND SUGGESTIONS FOR ADDITIONAL RESEARCH AND OTHER FOLLOW-UP

This study represents the beginning of an effort to examine the use of the criminal justice system as an intervention strategy for elder abuse. One purpose of the study was to determine the feasibility of building a predictor profile of elder abuse victims' willingness to prosecute their offspring abusers utilizing the data recorded on police complaint reports. As such, it focuses on the very beginning of the process of engagement between elder abuse victims and the police. Willingness to prosecute was defined as an important outcome variable as, in practical terms, it usually serves as the "gate" to ongoing engagement of the criminal justice system in the abuse situation.

Noted in Chapter II are the problems faced by researchers working outside the police department in tracking elder abuse cases that come to the attention of the police through the criminal justice system. To determine if the predictor profile developed as part of this study can serve to predict victims' stated willingness to prosecute their abusers, a follow-up study should be undertaken to determine if the findings hold with a different sample. As noted, the population examined in this study included 100% of elderly victims for whom complaint reports were filed with the NYPD in New York City in 1992 reflecting offenses committed against them by offspring.

Next, a sample of these victims would have to be tracked through the process of follow-up by a precinct-based detective, family or criminal court and/or the district attorney's office to determine the extent to which victims followed through with stated willingness to prosecute. In addition, an analysis would have to be performed to determine whether the predictor variables identified in this study also predicted follow-through with prosecution or whether other factors as yet undefined come into play as the process unfolds. Ultimately, a determination of the impact of victims' willingness to prosecute and actual prosecution on continued abuse by offspring would need to be made through a longitudinal study.

Both practice and program models need to continue to be developed and evaluated to ensure effective social work responsiveness to the problem of elder mistreatment and exploitation. This should include development and evaluation of models that involve collaboration between social workers and police: both to ensure effective intervention in elder abuse situations and to facilitate an ongoing dialogue between the disciplines of social work and criminal justice.

Appendices

Appendix A
NYPD Listing of Domestic Violence Related Offenses

DOMESTIC VIOLENCE REPORT
(State D.C.J.S.)

AGGRAVATED ASSAULT

P.D. CODE

109 Felonious Assault 1° & 2°

101 Assault 3° Weapons Codes A°B°C°D°E°F°H°J°K°M°P°.

SIMPLE ASSAULT

101 Assault 3° weapons codes G° & Z°

SEX OFFENSES

153 Rape 3°
155 Rape 2°
157 Rape 1° - Forcible
159 Rape 1° - Attempted Forcible

162 Consenual Sodomy
164 Sodomy 3°
166 Sodomy 2°
168 Sodomy 1°

170 Sexual Misconduct - Intercourse
174 Sexual Misconduct - Deviate

175 Sexual Abuse 2°
179 Sexual Abuse 1.°

693 Incest

OTHER OFFENSES

115 Reckless Endangerment 2°
117 Reckless Endangerment 1°

113 Menacing

637 Harassment Subdivision 1

NOTE: SEE PAGE 18 FOR WEAPONS CODES.

Appendix B
Additional Listing of Domestic Violence Offenses
(New York State Penal Code)

LISTING OF CRIMINAL OFFENSES RELATED TO ELDER ABUSE

1. Title H: Offenses against the person involving physical injury, sexual conduct, restraint and intimidation

120.00: Assault in 3rd degree

120.05: Assault in 2nd degree

120.10: Assault in 1st degree

120.15: Menacing

120.20: Reckless endangerment in 2nd degree

120.25: Reckless endangerment in 1st degree

120.30: Promoting a suicide attempt

120.35: Promoting a suicide attempt: by use of duress or deception

2. Article 125: Homicide and Related Offenses

125.10: Criminally negligent homicide: causes death of another person.

125.15: Manslaughter in 2nd degree

125.20: Manslaughter in 1st degree

125.25: Murder in 2nd degree

127.27: Murder in 1st degree

3. Sex Offenses Article 130

130.05: Sex offenses -lack of consent, forcible compulsion, incapacity to consent

130.20: sexual misconduct (sexual intercourse without consent)

130.35: Rape in 1st degree (forcible compulsion; physically helpless)

130.60: Sexual abuse in 2nd degree

130.65: Sexual abuse in 1st degree

130.70: Aggravated sexual abuse (insert object).

4. Coercion Article 135

135.05: Unlawful imprisonment in 2nd degree

135.10: Unlawful imprisonment in 1st degree: risk of serious harm

5. Title I. Offenses involving damages to and intrusion upon property

140 Burglary and related offenses

140.05 Trespass

145.15 Criminal trespass in 2nd degree

145.17 Criminal trespass in 1st degree

145 Criminal mischief and related offenses

145.00 Criminal mischief in 4th degree; 3rd degree; 2nd degree; 1st degree (145.12)

145.14 Criminal tampering in 3rd degree

145.25 Reckless endangerment of property

6. Title J: Offenses involving theft

150.00: Arson

155: Larceny/Extortion

o Grand larceny: 3rd degree
o Grand larceny 2nd degree
o grand larceny 1st degree

7. Article 160: Robbery

o Forcible larceny
o Forcible stealing
  - 3rd degree
  - 2nd degree
  - 1st degree

165: Misapplication (appropriation) of property

165.17: Unlawful use of credit or debit card

165.20: Fraudulently obtaining a signature

165.40: Criminal possession of stolen property
- 3rd Degree
- 2nd degree
- 1st degree

8. Title K: Offenses involving fraud

170: Forgery and related offenses

170.05: Forgery in 3rd degree

170.10: Forgery in 2nd degree

170.15: Forgery in 1st degree

175: Offenses involving false written statements

9. 190.60: Scheme to defraud (2nd degree)

190: Other fraud

10. 637 (?): Harassment

Appendix C
Sample NYPD Complaint Report

PAGE ___ OF ___ PAGES

Complaint Report PD 313-152 (Rev 3-84)-31

Complaint Report
PO 313-152 (Rev. 3-88)-31

Additional Copies For | 1 Jurisdiction | 3 | 8 Pct of Report | O.C.C.B No. | 12 Complaint No | PAGE ___ OF ___ PAGES | Fax No

Misery Time and Date of This Report | Time | 17 Date | Occurrence on or From | 23 Time | 27 Date | Day of Week | Occurrence Through | Time | Date | 33 | 14 PERP 1

Offense(s) If Any | P.L. Section | If fire related, was structure □ Occupied □ Vacant | If burglary, was entry forced □ Yes □ No □ Attempt | PERP 2

Victim
Last Name, First, M.I. | Address, include City, State, Zip | Apt No. | 15 PERP 1

Home Telephone | Business Telephone | Actions of Victim Prior to Robbery, Larceny or Sex Crimes | Aided/ Acc No. | PERP 2

34 Victim's Sex 1-Male 2-Female 3-Corp 4-State | 35 Age | Date of Birth | 37 Victim's Race 1-White 2-Black 3-Amer Ind 4-Asiatic 5-Hisp /White 6-Hisp /Black | 37A Living Together? 1-Yes 2-No | 38 Can Identify? B-If No, If yes, indicate if victim states perp is 1-Spouse 4-Parent / 6-Friend 2-Common Law Guardian 7-Stranger Spouse 5-Other 8-Other 3-Child Relative | 39 Comp. Rec'vd | Will View Photo? □ Yes □ No □ Unknown Will Prosecute? □ Yes □ No □ Unknown

Reporter/Witness
Reporter □ Witness □ Last Name, First | Address, include City, State, Zip | Apt No. | 16 DHOE 1

Home Telephone | Business Telephone | Position / Relationship | Sex | Race | Date of Birth | Age | DHOE 2

Type of Location (Specific) | 40 Address / Location of Occurrence | 41 Sec / Post of Occ. | 44 Visible by Patrol 1 □ Yes 2 □ No

45 | 48 | 49 | 50 | 51 | 52 | 53 Pct of Arrest | 56 Arrest No.'s | 61 Rep. Ag'cy Code | PDU Case No. | 17 DHOE 1

Evidence | Voucher No. | Case Status □ Open □ Closed | Unit Referred To | Log No. | DHOE 2

Vehicle
Plate □ Lost □ Stolen | License No. | State | Exp. | Type | No of Plates | Vin No. | 18 DHOE 1

Year | Make | Model | Style | Color | Value | Ins. Code | Policy No. | Larceny of Motor Vehicle Only P-Parking Lot D-Public Garage J-Street M-Other | DHOE 2

Voucher No. | Vehicle was □ Used in Crime □ Stolen | Alarm No. | Pct | Time | Date

Property
LOST □ STOLEN □ | If stolen, was property □ Business □ Personal □ Both | Owner identification No.

Quantity | Article | Description-Brand, Model, Serial No.

Property Summary

Item	64	65 Value Stolen	72 Value Recovered
Motor Vehicle Stolen-Rec'x	81		
M V Recv'x By Dr For Other Auth	82		
Currency	84		
Jewelry	85		
Furs, Clothing	86		
Firearms	87		
Office Equib	88		
TV's Radios Cameras	89		
Household Goods	10		
Consumables	11		
Misc.	13		

4 PERP 1 | 19 DHOE 1
PERP 2
5 PERP 1 | DHOE 2
PERP 2
6 PERP 1 | 20 PERP 1

Perpetrators

Total No. of Perpetrators | Wanted □ | Arrested □ | Weapon □ Used □ Possessed | Describe Weapon (If firearm, give color, make, calibre, type, model, etc.) | 21 PERP 1

Perp. No. 1
Wanted □ | Arrested □ | Last Name, First, M.I. | Address, include City, State, Zip | Apt No. | Res. Pct.

Sex | Race | Date of Birth | Age | Height Ft. In. | Weight | Eye Color | Hair Color | Hair Length | Facial Hair | Accent

□ Eyeglasses □ Sunglasses | Clothing Description. | 22 PERP 1

Nickname, First Name, Alias | Scars, Marks, M.O., Etc. (Continue In "Details"):

Perp. No. 2
Wanted □ | Arrested □ | Last Name, First, M.I. | Address, include City, State, Zip | Apt No. | Res. Pct.

Sex | Race | Date of Birth | Age | Height Ft. In. | Weight | Eye Color | Hair Color | Hair Length | Facial Hair | Accent

□ Eyeglasses □ Sunglasses | Clothing Description. | 23 PERP 1

Nickname, First Name, Alias | Scars, Marks, M.O., Etc. (Continue In "Details"):

List Additional Victims & Witnesses — Reconstruct Occurrence including Method of Entry & Escape — Include Unique or Unusual Actions

24

Appendix D
Letter from Human Resources
Commisioner Barebara J. Sabol to
New York City Police Commissioner
Raymond Kelly Requesting Access to
Complaint Reports

HUMAN RESOURCES ADMINISTRATION
250 CHURCH STREET, NEW YORK, N.Y. 10013

BARBARA J. SABOL
Administrator/Commissioner

October 1, 1992

Raymond Kelly
Acting Commissioner
New York Police Department
One Police Plaza New York, New York 10007

Dear Commissioner Kelly:

I write to request the cooperation and assistance of the Police
Department in a study to be undertaken by the Human Resources
Administration (HRA) of older victims of domestic abuse by
children and grandchildren. As you know, HRA provides entitlements, case management services, Medicaid funded home care and
protective services to thousands of older adults (age 60 and
above). The phenomenon of elder abuse, as described in the lead
article in <u>Newsday</u>, Sunday, September 13, 1992, is perceived as
an increasing problem for older New Yorkers on HRA's caseload.

HRA is planning to undertake a study designed to learn more about
victims of elder abuse and the circumstances under which they may
or may not be willing to prosecute their abusers after reporting
the abuse incident to the police. We believe the findings,
including descriptive data, will be valuable in assisting HRA to
more effectively target services to victims of elder abuse.
Patricia Brownell, Manager, Special Projects, for Mary Nakashian,
Executive Deputy Commissioner, Family Support Administration,
HRA, and a doctoral candidate at the Fordham University School of
Social Work, has been assigned to undertake this study. Richard
O'Halleron, Acting Deputy General Counsel for the HRA Office of
Legal Affairs and expert on elder abuse, will serve as HRA
advisor to this study. Dr. Joseph Ryan, who is on the New York
Police Department (NYPD) staff and has represented the NYPD on
the Elder Abuse Coalition, is Ms. Brownell's dissertation advisor. Dr. Ryan has expressed considerable interest in this
project and believes the findings will be useful to NYPD as well
as HRA.

The proposed study is intended to examine the relationship
between abuse of older adults (age 60 and above) by offspring and
the criminal justice system, and the availability of the criminal
justice system as an intervention strategy for this form of
domestic violence. In order for Ms. Brownell to undertake this
study on behalf of the agency, the Police Department would have
to identify a random sample of 350 crime reports involving
victims age 60 and above who have reported in 1991 a criminal act
against them by an offspring. Patricia Henry, Director, Program
Planning, Office of the Deputy Mayor for Public Safety, has

confirmed the willingness of that office to provide support to
this project, in order to facilitate access to records. Ms.
Henry is sending you a letter under separate cover acknowledging
this arrangement.

Too often, older clients will not take action necessary to
protect themselves if they are abused by loved ones who are their
offspring. Work with battered spouses has demonstrated that the
police are the most valuable first line of defense against
ongoing violence by family members. The family and criminal
courts can also provide protection for victims of domestic
violence. To engage the court system, however, abuse victims must
be willing to prosecute their abusers. Persuading them to do so
is a challenge not only to the police - who may receive the
initial call for assistance from the victim - but also to social
workers from HRA. Often this willingness on the part of the
victim is critical to HRA's legal staff, who evaluate taking
civil and criminal interventions to protect these victims served
by protective services and other HRA-administered programs.

I look forward to reviewing the findings of this study, as well
as implications for increased collaboration between the Police
Department and HRA in addressing elder abuse on the HRA caseload.
If your staff have questions or require additional information,
you may advise them to contact Patricia Brownell, Family Support
Administration Executive Office, 250 Church Street, Room 1408, at
(212) 274-2614 or 274-2621.

Thank you for giving serious consideration to this request.

Sincerely,

Barbara J. Sabol

cc. M. Nakashian ✓
    J. Capoziello

Appendix E
Letter from New York City Police Department Liaison Sergeant Daniel Parente Accompanying Requested Complaint Reports for Research Study

POLICE DEPARTMENT

NEW YORK, N.Y. 10038   374-5367

February 19, 1993

Pat Brownell
Manager, Special Projects
Human Resources Administration
Family Support Administration
250 Church Street, New York, N.Y. 10013

Dear Ms. Brownell:

        Enclosed are copies of 318 complaint reports,
as you have requested, for your study on elder abuse. As we have
previously discussed, information has been redacted from these
reports pursuant to our Legal Bureau's direction. However, there
still should be sufficient data on these reports to enable you to
perform your study. If there or any problems or if I can be of
any further assistance please feel free to contact me at (2120
374-5367.

                                  Sincerely,

                                  Daniel Parente
                                  Sergeant
                                  Office of Management
                                  Analysis and Planning

enclosure

Appendix F
Sample Data Entry Form with Coding Criteria

<u>ABUSE OF ELDERLY PARENTS BY THEIR CHILDREN</u>: Data Collection Sheet

/_/_/_/   Record Number
(1-3)

_/   Type of Abuse (High Intensity: non-sexual)
(4)   (High Intensity: sexual)
                        (Low Intensity)
                        (Financial)

-/_/_/   Age of Victim
(5-7)

_/   Sex of Victim (M) (F)
(8)

_/   Victim Lives with Abuser (Yes) (No) (Other)
(9)

_/   Relatedness of Abuser to Victim (Son) (Daughter) (Son-in
              law) (Daughter-in-law) (Step-son) (Step-daughter)
              (Grandson) (Granddaughter) (Other)
(10)

_/   Victim Reporting Abuse to Police (Victim report) (Other)
(11)

_/   Gender of Abuser (M) (F)
(12)

_/_/   Age of Abuser
(13-14)

_/   Race/Ethnicity of Victim (White) (Black) (Amer. Ind.)
              (Asian) (Hisp. White) (Hisp. Black)
(15)

_/   Abuser also substance abuser (Yes) (No) (Unknown)
              (Missing)
(16)

_/   Victim Willing to Prosecute Abuser (Yes) (No).
(17)

-/_/_/   Number of Precinct
(18-19)

Appendix G
Addenda on Precinct/Community Board Data

ADDENDUM: PRECINCT DATA

o Breakdown of complaint reports and ethnicity of victim/abuser
  by precinct

o Map of Manhattan with police precincts

o Map of Manhattan Community Districts with descriptions

Please note that in Manhattan, police precincts and community
boards are only co-terminous above 59th Street. Below 59th Street,
police precincts are defined by zip codes. Listed below are the
police precincts in Manhattan and the community boards that they
cover. This information is provided as census data on populations
(including populations 60 years and above) are compiled by
community board.

Precinct	Community Boards
1	1/2
5	3
6	2
7	3
9	3
10	4/5
13	5/6
17	6
Manhat North	4
Manhat South	4/5

----------------------------Co-terminous Above 59th Street

19	8
20	7
23	11
24	7
25	11
26	9
28	10
30	9

32 10

34 12

BREAKDOWN OF ABUSE COMPLAINT REPORTS BY PRECINCT AND ETHNICITY
FOR SAMPLE OF 295 ABUSE REPORTS

o 1/2: Tribeca/Wall Street
   Three reports (1.0%): 3 Black
o 5: Chinatown/Little Italy
   One report (.3%): White
o 6: Greenwich Village
   One report (.3%): White
o 7: Lower East Side
   Twelve (12) reports (4.1%): 6 White, 4 Hispanic, 2 Black
o 9: East Village
   Twelve (12) reports (4.1%): 6 Hispanic, 5 White, 1 Black
o 10: Chelsea
   Three reports (1.0%): 2 White, 1 Black
o 13: Grammercy
   Three reports (1.0%): 3 White
o 14: Midtown South
   Five reports (1.7%): 2 White, 2 Hispanic, 1 Black
o 17: Midtown
   One report (.3%): White
o 18: Midtown North
   Eleven (11) reports (3.7%): 6 White, 3 Hispanic, 1 Black)
o 19: East Side
   Seventeen (17) reports (5.8%): 17 White
o 20: West Side
   Six reports (2.0%): 3 Hispanic, 2 White, 1 Black
o 23: Upper East Side
   Forty (40) reports (13.6%): 25 Black, 15 Hispanic
o 24: Upper West Side
   Twenty-four (24) reports (13.6%): 10 White, 9 Black, 5 Hispanic
o 25: East Harlem
   Thirty-one (31) reports (10.5%): 20 Black, 9 Hispanic, 1 White
o 26: Morningside Heights
   Eight reports (2.7%): 4 Black, 4 Hispanic
o 28: Central Harlem
   Thirty (30) reports (10.2%): 29 Black, 1 Hispanic
o 30: Harlem (by Riverside Drive)
   Twenty (20) reports (6.8%): 16 Black, 4 Hispanic
o 32: Harlem (above Central Harlem)
   Forty-six (46) reports (15.6%): 44 Black, 1 White, 1 Hispanic
o 34: Washington Heights
   Twenty-one (21) reports (7.1%): 12 Hispanic, 8 Black, 1 Asian

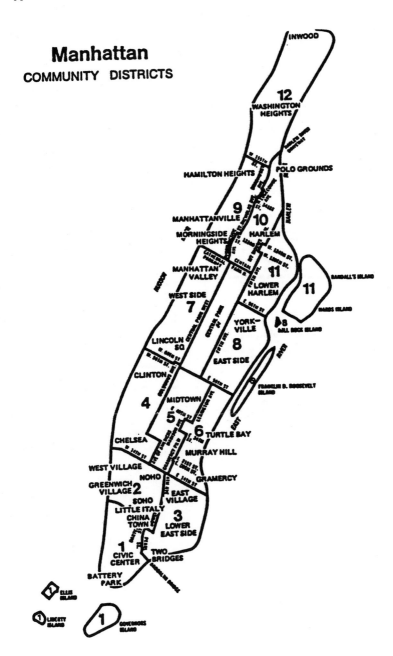

Manhattan
COMMUNITY DISTRICTS

MANHATTAN COMMUNITY DISTRICTS
BOUNDED AS FOLLOWS

District 1
North: Canal Street
East: Baxter Street, A New Street, Pearl Street, Brooklyn Bridge, East River
South: Upper New York Bay (includes Governors Island, Liberty Island, Ellis Island)
West: Hudson River

District 2
North: West 14th Street, East 14th Street
East: Bowery, Fourth Avenue
South: Canal Street
West: Hudson River

District 3
North: East 14th Street
East: East River
South: Brooklyn Bridge
West: Pearl Street, A New Street, Baxter Street, Canal Street, Bowery, Fourth Avenue

District 4
North: West 59th Street, Columbus Avenue, West 60th Street
East: Northern and Eastern Boundary of Columbus Circle, Eighth Avenue, West 26th Street, Avenue of the Americas
South: West 14th Street
West: Hudson River

District 5
North: Central Park South, East 59th Street
East: Lexington Avenue, East 40th Street, Madison Avenue, East 34th Street, Lexington Avenue, East 21st Street, Gramercy Park West, East 20th Street, Irving Place
South: East 14th Street, West 14th Street
West: Avenue of the Americas, West 26th Street, Eighth Avenue, Southeastern Boundary of Columbus Circle

District 6
North: East 59th Street
East: East River
South: East 14th Street
West: Irving Place, East 20th Street, Gramercy Park West, East 21st Street, Lexington Avenue, East 34th Street, Madison Avenue, East 40th Street, Lexington Avenue

District 7
North: Cathedral Parkway
East: Central Park West
South: Northern Boundary of Columbus Circle, West 60th Street, Columbus Avenue, West 59th Street
West: Hudson River

District 8
North: East 96th Street
East: East River (District includes Mill Rock Island, Franklin D. Roosevelt Island)
South: East 59th Street
West: Fifth Avenue

District 9
North: West 155th Street
East: Edgecombe Avenue, West 145th Street, Bradhurst Avenue, West 141st Street, St. Nicholas Avenue, Manhattan Avenue, West 123rd Street, Morningside Avenue, Manhattan Avenue
South: Cathedral Parkway
West: Hudson River

District 10
North: Harlem River
East: Fifth Avenue, West 124th Street, Mount Morris Park West, West 120th Street, Fifth Avenue
South: Central Park North
West: Manhattan Avenue, Morningside Avenue, West 123rd Street, Manhattan Avenue, St. Nicholas Avenue, West 141st Street, Bradhurst Avenue, West 145th Street, Edgecombe Avenue, Harlem River Driveway

District 11
North: Harlem River
East: East River (including Randall's and Wards Island)
South: East 96th Street
West: Fifth Avenue, West 120th Street, Mt. Morris Park West, West 124th Street, Fifth Avenue

District 12
North: Harlem River
East: Harlem River, Harlem River Driveway
South: West 155th Street
West: Hudson River

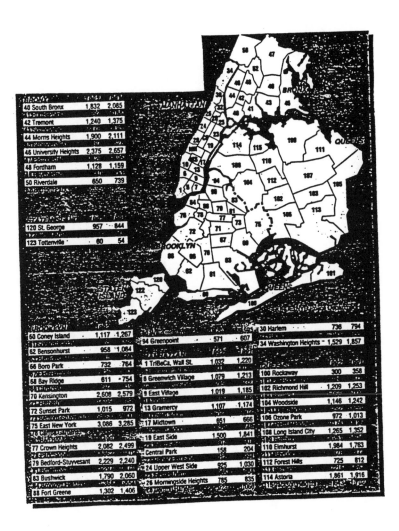

BRONX

40 South Bronx	1,832	2,085
42 Tremont	1,240	1,375
44 Morris Heights	1,900	2,111
46 University Heights	2,375	2,657
48 Fordham	1,128	1,159
50 Riverdale	650	739

STATEN ISLAND

120 St. George	957	844
123 Tottenville	60	54

BROOKLYN

60 Coney Island	1,117	1,267
62 Bensonhurst	958	1,084
66 Boro Park	732	764
68 Bay Ridge	611	754
70 Kensington	2,608	2,579
72 Sunset Park	1,015	972
75 East New York	3,086	3,285
77 Crown Heights	2,082	2,499
79 Bedford-Stuyvesant	2,229	2,240
83 Bushwick	1,790	2,060
88 Fort Greene	1,302	1,406

94 Greenpoint	571	607

MANHATTAN

1 TriBeCa, Wall St.	1,032	1,220
6 Greenwich Village	1,079	1,213
9 East Village	1,019	1,185
13 Gramercy	1,107	1,174
17 Midtown	651	666
19 East Side	1,500	1,841
Central Park	158	204
24 Upper West Side	925	1,030
26 Morningside Heights	785	835
30 Harlem	736	794
34 Washington Heights	1,529	1,857

QUEENS

100 Rockaway	300	358
102 Richmond Hill	1,209	1,253
104 Woodside	1,146	1,242
106 Ozone Park	972	1,013
108 Long Island City	1,265	1,352
110 Elmhurst	1,984	1,763
112 Forest Hills	725	812
114 Astoria	1,861	1,916

Appendix H
Description of Sample of 295
Abuse Reports and Categories of
Abuse by Offenses

The sample used to test the above hypothesis is a subset of the 295 complaint reports described in Chapter IV. This sample was identified according to whether information on willingness to prosecute was included on the complaint report. A total for 238 complaint reports included information on willingness to prosecute.

Based on an analysis of the subset of complaint reports that included information on willingness to prosecute compared with the total set of reports, it is determined that the sample reflects reports where the information on willingness to prosecute was omitted at random. It was not found to be due to a systemic bias on the part of police officers completing the reports. Included here is the analysis of the complete sample of 295 abuse reports.

Age of victims. The age of the victims in the sample ranged from 60 to 93 years of age, with a mean of 69 and a standard deviation of 7. Of these, 239 (81%) were aged 60 to 74 years and 56 (19%) were 75 years and above.

Age of abusers. The age of the abusers ranged from 13 to 69 years of age. The mean age of the abusers was 34 years with a standard deviation of 10.

Gender of victims. The victims in the sample were predominantly female (217 or 74%) as opposed to male (72 or 26%).

Gender of abusers. The abusers in the sample were predominantly male (235 or 80% male as opposed to 60 or 20% female).

Race/ethnicity. Because the sample reflects offspring abuse, it is assumed that both victim and abuser are the same race/ethnicity. The sample included 59 (20%) whites, 165 or 56% blacks, 1 or .3% Asian, and 69 or 23% Hispanic victims/abusers.

Relationship between victims and abusers. Abusers of elders in the sample included 231 (78%) sons, 55 (19%) daughters, 1 (.3%) stepson, 2 (.78) stepdaughters, 5 (1.7%) grandsons, 1 (.3%) granddaughter, 1 (.3%) daughter-in-law, and 1 (.3%) nephew.

Living arrangements between victims and abusers. The majority of the victims identified in the sample lived with their abusers: 150 (51%) lived with their abusers as opposed to 128 (43%) who did not. Of the 295 complaint reports, 17 (6%) did not include information on living arrangements between victims and abusers.

Reporter to police. The majority of the victims in the sample self-reported the abuse to the police (264 or 90% as opposed to 31 or 10% who did not).

Category (type) of abuse. Based on the categories defined by Pillemer and Wolf (physical, financial, and psychological), types of abuse reflected in the complaint reports reviewed in the study included 87 (30%) reports of physical abuse, 97 (33%) reports of financial abuse, and 111 (38%) psychological abuse.

Intensity of abuse. Based on the classification scheme adapted from the Uniform Crime Report (U.S. Department of Justice), the offenses reflected in the sample were recoded into low- and high-intensity abuse. Low-intensity abuse was recorded in 212 (72%) of the complaint reports and high-intensity abuse was recorded in 83 (28%) of the sample complaint reports.

Willingness to prosecute. The majority of elder abuse victims in the sample stated willingness to prosecute (176 or 60%) as opposed to unwillingness to prosecute (62 or 21%). In the larger sample of 295 discussed here, 57 or 19% of complaint reports did not include information on victims' willingness to prosecute.

Abusers' substance abuse. In the sample of 295, 42 or 14% of complaint reports contained information indicating the abuser was a substance abuser; in 253 or 86% of the reports, information on this was missing.

Appendix I
NYPD Patrol Guide:
FamilyOffenses/Domestic Violence
Procedure No. 110-38;
Revision No. 89-8

PATROL GUIDE

	PROCEDURE No	110-38

FAMILY OFFENSES/DOMESTIC VIOLENCE

DATE ISSUED	DATE EFFECTIVE	REVISION NUMBER	PAGE
10-6-89	10-13-89	89-8	1 of 6

PURPOSE   To process family offenses and domestic violence that occur between family members.

Misc. 1953-F (11-89-14

DEFINITIONS   **COMPLAINANT/VICTIM** - For purposes of this procedure ONLY, is limited to a person described in subdivisions "a" through "g" below.
FAMILY/HOUSEHOLD - AS DEFINED IN FAMILY COURT ACT - includes persons who:
a. Are legally married to one another
b. Are related by blood (consanguinity)
c. Were formerly legally married to one another
d. Are related by marriage (affinity)
e. Have a child in common regardless of whether such persons have been married or have lived together at any time.
FAMILY/HOUSEHOLD - EXPANDED DEFINITION - includes subdivisions "a" through "e" above, AND persons who:
f. Are not legally married, but are currently living together in a family-type relationship
g. Are not legally married, but formerly lived together in a family-type relationship.
A family/household thus includes "common-law" marriages, same sex couples, different generations of the same family, siblings and in-laws.

FAMILY OFFENSE - Any act which may constitute disorderly conduct (including acts amounting to disorderly conduct NOT committed in a public place), harassment, menacing, reckless endangerment, assault 2nd or 3rd degree, or attempted assault between members of the same family/household, AS DEFINED IN THE FAMILY COURT ACT (subdivisions "a" through "e" above). If the offense is OTHER THAN one of the foregoing, and/or the family/household relationship is NOT one defined in the Family Court Act, the offense IS NOT A FAMILY OFFENSE and must be processed in Criminal Court.

PROBABLE CAUSE - A combination of facts, viewed through the eyes of a police officer, which would lead a person of reasonable caution to believe that a crime is being or has been committed. The "probable cause" standard applied in family offense/domestic violence offenses is no different from the standard applied in other offenses.

ORDER OF PROTECTION - An order issued by the Criminal Court, Family Court, or the Supreme Court, requiring compliance with specific conditions of behavior, hours of visitation and any other condition deemed appropriate by the court of issuance. An Order of Protection may also be issued by the Supreme Court as part of a separation decree, divorce judgment, annulment, or as part of a court order in a pending separation, divorce or annulment action. Failure to comply with the terms of an Order of Protection is a misdemeanor.

LEGAL REFERENCES
Section 153b, Family Court Act
Section 168, Family Court Act
Section 812, Family Court Act
Section 846-A, Family Court Act
Section 847, Family Court Act
Section 215.50, Penal Law
Section 530.11, Criminal Procedure Law
Section 530.12, Criminal Procedure Law
Section 530.13, Criminal Procedure Law
Section 420, Social Services Law
Section 252, Domestic Relations Law

PATROL GUIDE

PROCEDURE No.

110-38

FAMILY OFFENSES/DOMESTIC VIOLENCE

DATE ISSUED 10-6-89	DATE EFFECTIVE 10-13-89	REVISION NUMBER 89-8	PAGE 2 of 6

PROCEDURE
When a report of ANY OFFENSE committed between members of the same family/household, as described in the EXPANDED DEFINITION, is brought to the attention of a uniformed member of the service or the member is directed to respond to such offense by competent authority:

UNIFORMED
MEMBER OF
THE SERVICE
1. Ascertain all facts.
2. Obtain medical assistance if requested or the need is apparent.
3. Determine whether there are children present in the home who may be victims of neglect/abuse/maltreatment:
   a. If a member REASONABLY SUSPECTS a child less than eighteen (18) is abused, neglected or maltreated, prepare REPORT OF SUSPECTED CHILD ABUSE OR MALTREATMENT (PD377-154); notify the State Central Registry, and/or take other appropriate action as outlined in Patrol Guide procedure 106-15.

NOTE
Willful failure to make such notification is a Class "A" Misdemeanor. Further, civil liability may result for the damages caused by such failure.

4. Determine whether:
   a. Probable cause exists that any offense has been committed
   b. Order of Protection has been obtained by complainant/victim.

NOTE
A COMPLAINT REPORT (PD313-152) WILL BE PREPARED IN ALL CASES in which police respond to any alleged offenses, including instances of failure to comply with the terms of an Order of Protection, committed between members of the same family/household, as described in the EXPANDED DEFINITION. If the underlying act which violates the Order of Protection is not a crime, the offense to be listed in the "OFFENSE" captions on the COMPLAINT REPORT and the COMPLAINT INDEX (PD313-141) is "Violation of Order of Protection." Under the "DETAILS" section of the COMPLAINT REPORT indicate the court that issued the Order of Protection.

WHERE THERE IS PROBABLE CAUSE THAT A FELONY HAS BEEN COMMITTED OR AN INDIVIDUAL FAILS TO COMPLY WITH THE TERMS OF AN ORDER OF PROTECTION:
5. Arrest offender even if complainant/victim does **not** want offender arrested.

WHEN COMPLAINANT/VICTIM INDICATES THAT AN ORDER OF PROTECTION HAS BEEN OBTAINED:
6. Request complainant/victim to produce Order of Protection.
   a. If Order of Protection cannot be produced, telephone Central Records Division, Identification Section, to verify that Order of Protection was issued, court of issuance, specific conduct prohibited by Order of Protection and the expiration date.

NOTE
Central Records Division maintains a file of Orders of Protection and will respond to telephone inquiries concerning such Orders of Protection twenty-four (24) hours a day. If Central Records Division does not have an Order of Protection on file, check with the desk officer to determine whether Order of Protection has been filed at precinct level. In those instances in which an Order of Protection is delivered to a station house, the desk officer will make an entry in the Command Log and forward the Order of Protection to the Central Records Division, Identification Section, for file. Amendments to, and revocations of, such Orders of Protection will also be forwarded.

PATROL GUIDE

PROCEDURE No.   110-38

FAMILY OFFENSES/DOMESTIC VIOLENCE

DATE ISSUED	DATE EFFECTIVE	REVISION NUMBER	PAGE
10-6-89	10-13-89	89-8	3 of 6

Misc. 1983-F (11-88-14

WHEN THERE IS PROBABLE CAUSE THAT A MISDEMEANOR, OTHER THAN AN ACT THAT FAILS TO COMPLY WITH AN ORDER OF PROTECTION, HAS BEEN COMMITTED, EITHER IN OR OUT OF THE OFFICER'S PRESENCE, OR THAT ANY VIOLATION HAS BEEN COMMITTED IN THE OFFICER'S PRESENCE:

7. Arrest offender IF complainant/victim wants offender arrested.
   a. When complainant/victim does NOT want offender arrested and/
      or indicates reluctance to prosecute, it is within the
      officer's discretion to effect the arrest, IF in his/her
      judgment, an arrest is warranted.

NOTE   Officer is required to make an arrest as specified in steps 5 and/or
       7, even though:
       a. The parties are married, or are members of the same family/house-
          hold, as described in the EXPANDED DEFINITION, OR
       b. The complainant/victim has not sought or obtained an Order of Pro-
          tection, OR
       c. The officer believes that complainant/victim will not sign a com-
          plaint in court, OR
       d. The complainant/victim has instituted prior pending legal proceed-
          ings, OR
       e. The officer prefers to act as mediator or reconcile the differ-
          ences between the parties, OR
       f. The complainant/victim does not have visible injuries.

8. Make ACTIVITY LOG (PD112-145) entry if complainant/victim does not
   want arrest effected for a misdemeanor or any violation committed
   in the officer's presence by family member as outlined in this
   procedure:
   a. Request complainant/victim to sign entry
   b. Enter "REFUSED SIGNATURE" if complainant/victim will not sign
      entry.

IF THERE IS PROBABLE CAUSE THAT ANY VIOLATION HAS BEEN COMMITTED, NOT IN THE OFFICER'S PRESENCE:

9. Refer complainant/victim to Summons Part, Criminal Court.
   a.   346 Broadway in all boroughs, EXCEPT Staten Island
   b.   67 Targee Street in Staten Island.

NOTE   Officer cannot effect an arrest for a VIOLATION NOT COMMITTED IN HIS/
       HER PRESENCE, UNLESS the conduct constituting such violation is spe-
       cifically prohibited in existing, current Order of Protection issued
       to the complainant/victim.

10. Advise complainant/victim of availability of shelter and other
    services.
    a. Provide complainant/victim with form RIGHTS OF VICTIMS OF
       FAMILY OFFENSES (PD154-120).
11. Remain at scene in NON-ARREST situation until satisfied that
    danger of recurrence of dispute has subsided.

UPON ARREST OF OFFENDER

12. Ascertain whether act for which arrest is made constitutes a
    Family Offense.

PATROL GUIDE

PROCEDURE No.   110-38

FAMILY OFFENSES/DOMESTIC VIOLENCE

DATE ISSUED	DATE EFFECTIVE	REVISION NUMBER	PAGE
10-6-89	10-13-89	89-8	4 of 6

Misc. 1053-F (11-88-14

NOTE   To constitute a Family Offense, two (2) conditions MUST BE MET, to wit: the specific offense AND family/household relationship between victim and offender MUST be as specified in Family Court Act (refer to definition of Family Offense, at beginning of procedure). If either condition is NOT MET, the offense is NOT a Family Offense and MUST be processed in Criminal Court.

13. Determine court jurisdiction, as follows:
   a. Family Offenses - Family Court and Criminal Court have concurrent jurisdiction; charge(s) may be processed in either Family Court or Criminal Court.
   b. Non-Family Offenses (includes Assault 1st Degree) - Criminal Court has exclusive jurisdiction; charge(s) must be processed in Criminal Court.
   c. Criminal charge, OTHER THAN A FAMILY OFFENSE, is alleged, IN ADDITION TO a charge that may be processed by the Family Court - ALL CHARGES MUST BE BROUGHT TO CRIMINAL COURT FOR PROCESSING.

NOTE   When the act is a failure to comply with an Order of Protection and is also a:
-Crime (non-family offense) - violator MUST be charged with that crime. The violator will be brought to Criminal Court regardless of which court issued the Order of Protection.
-Family Offense - concurrent jurisdiction exists regardless of which court issued the Order of Protection.

An act which normally would not constitute an offense, but which is prohibited by and would fail to comply with the terms of an Order of Protection, e.g., going to complainant's residence or place of employment, telephoning the complainant, etc., can only be prosecuted in the court that issued the Order of Protection.

If the underlying act is a failure to comply with the terms of an Order of Protection and is not a crime, the offense to be listed on the ON LINE BOOKING SYSTEM ARREST WORKSHEET (PD244-159) is "Violation of Order of Protection." If the Order of Protection emanates from Family Court, it is an "Unclassified Misdemeanor" under Section 846-A of the Family Court Act. If Criminal Court Order of Protection, it is a "A" Misdemeanor under Section 215.50 of the Penal Law.

WHEN CONCURRENT JURISDICTION EXISTS:
14. Advise complainant/victim that:
   a. Criminal Court processing of the charge(s) is for the purpose of prosecution of the offender and may result in a criminal conviction.
   b. Family Court processing of the charge(s) is a civil proceeding, the purpose of which is to attempt to stop the violence, end family disruption, and provide protection. Counselling is also available.
   c. Charges may be brought in either court and that complainant/victim has option to change from one court to the other, within seventy-two (72) hours, after commencement of actual court proceedings, IF case has not been adjudicated within such time.

PATROL GUIDE

PROCEDURE No   110-38

FAMILY OFFENSES/DOMESTIC VIOLENCE			
DATE ISSUED	DATE EFFECTIVE	REVISION NUMBER	PAGE
10-6-89	10-13-89	89-8	5 of 6

UNIFORMED
MEMBER OF
THE SERVICE
(continued)

    d. Both Criminal and Family Court have the authority to issue an Order of Protection, the purpose of which is to stop the violence and provide protection.

15. Make entry in ACTIVITY LOG indicating that complainant/victim was advised of:
    a. Difference between proceedings in each court
    b. Importance in selection of appropriate court to process charge(s) and option to change from one court to the other under specific circumstances.

16. DO NOT issue DESK APPEARANCE TICKET (PD260-121) when complainant/victim and offender are members of the same family/household, as defined in the EXPANDED DEFINITION of family/household at beginning of procedure, AND:
    a. Offender failed to comply with an Order of Protection
    b. Offense charged is disorderly conduct (including acts amounting to disorderly conduct not committed in a public place, harassment, menacing, reckless endangerment 2nd degree, assault 3rd degree, or attempted assault
    c. Complainant/victim requests opportunity to obtain a Temporary Order of Protection, or facts of the case indicate the immediate need of a Temporary Order of Protection because of strong possibility of recurrence of violence against complainant/victim (e.g., past history of assaults against complainant/victim, statements made by defendant, active present hostility against complainant/victim, etc.)
    d. Issuance is prohibited by any other provision of Patrol Guide procedure 110-16 (DESK APPEARANCE TICKETS-GENERAL PROCEDURES)

NOTE

Violator will not be released on station house bail if not eligible for a Desk Appearance Ticket as per criteria listed in step 16, above.

DESK
OFFICER

17. Verify accuracy and completeness of all required forms.
18. Have prisoner removed to appropriate central booking facility to complete arrest process.

WHEN OFFENDER HAS DEPARTED SCENE PRIOR TO ARRIVAL OF POLICE:

UNIFORMED
MEMBER OF
THE SERVICE

19. Conduct search of immediate vicinity for offender when:
    a. Probable cause exists that a crime has been committed or an Order of Protection has been violated, AND
    b. Officer has reason to believe that such search may be fruitful.
20. Advise complainant/victim to call police when offender returns, if search produces no results.

WHEN NO ARREST IS MADE:

21. Prepare COMPLAINT REPORT, in all instances when no arrest is made, including any act which fails to comply with an Order of Protection, committed by absent offender.
    a. Include under "Details", the possible location of the absent offender, if known (e.g., home of friend or place of employment, etc.)

PATROL GUIDE

PROCEDURE No. 110-38

FAMILY OFFENSES/DOMESTIC VIOLENCE

DATE ISSUED	DATE EFFECTIVE	REVISION NUMBER	PAGE
10-6-89	10-13-89	89-8	6 of 6

UNIFORMED MEMBER OF THE SERVICE (continued)

b. Appropriate entry <u>must</u> be made on COMPLAINT REPORT in box captioned "Unit Referred To", i.e., Detective Squad, Summons Part - Criminal Court or Family Court. If the offense is a felony, or any act which violates the conditions of an Order of Protection or a complainant/victim wants the offender arrested for committing a misdemeanor, refer COMPLAINT REPORT to detective squad.

NOTE

Whenever a COMPLAINT REPORT is forwarded to the detective squad for a felony or a misdemeanor and there is an active Order of Protection, the member preparing the COMPLAINT REPORT <u>must</u> indicate under the details section of the REPORT the following: <u>"Order of Protection is in effect."</u>

22. Refer complainant/victim, when no arrest is made, as follows:
   a. Family/household members as defined in Family Court Act to:
     (1) Family Court OR
     (2) Summons Part - Criminal Court
   b. Family/household-expanded definition subdivisions "f" and "g", i.e., "Are not legally married but are currently living together in a family type relationship" or "Are not legally married but formerly lived together in family type relationship."
     (1) Summons Part - Criminal Court.

ADDITIONAL DATA

Communications Division personnel will assign past family disputes (radio code signal 10-52, D-6) to available SP10 Units through the "FINEST" System, <u>only when</u> the offender is no longer on the scene <u>and</u> no weapon, violence or crime is involved. If no SP10 Unit is working in the precinct of occurrence, all past family disputes, as indicated above, as well as all other family disputes, and Order of Protection situations, will be assigned by the radio dispatcher to precinct radio motor patrol units in the usual manner.

A police officer may be required to assist in serving a summons, a petition, or a Temporary Order of Protection in conformance with the Family Court Act.

To avoid unnecessary court appearances by uniformed members of the service who are requested by a petitioner to serve a respondent with a summons, petition or Temporary Order of Protection as required by the Family Court Act (Section 153b), the uniformed member of the service will prepare STATEMENT OF PERSONAL SERVICE (PD260-152). The uniformed member concerned will sign the STATEMENT OF PERSONAL SERVICE after completing <u>all</u> captions on the form. It is no longer sworn to before a supervisory officer. The original copy (white) will be given <u>to the petitioner and the duplicate copy (blue) will be filed in the precinct of service.</u>

RELATED PROCEDURES

Emergency Removals or Investigation and Reporting of Abused, Neglected or Maltreated Children (P.G. 106-15)
Arrest - General (P.G. 110-2)
Desk Appearance Ticket - General Procedure (P.G. 110-16)
Unlawful Evictions (P.G. 117-11)

Bibliography

Abelman, I. (1992). *Report on incidence of adult abuse on the protective services for adults caseload in New York City*. Unpublished report, New York State Department of Social Services.

American Society on Aging. (1991, October-November). Research and practice: Understanding diversity is key to helping abused elders. *Aging Today* (The Bi-monthly Newsletter of the American Society on Aging), p. 14.

Anetzburger, G. (1987). *The etiology of elder abuse by adult offspring.* Springfield, IL: Chas. C. Thomas.

Block, M. R., & Sinnott, J. D. (Eds.). (1979). *The battered syndrome: An exploratory study.* College Park, MD: University of Maryland Center on Aging.

Breckman, R., & Adelman, R. (1988). *Strategies for interventions into elder mistreatment.* Newbury, CA: Sage Press.

Brown, A. (1989). A survey on elder abuse at one native American tribe. *Journal of Elder Abuse and Neglect 1*(2), 17-37.

Brownell, P. (1990). *Elder abuse as a form of domestic violence.* Unpublished study.

Cantor, M. (1993). *Growing older in New York City in the 1990's: A study of changing lifestyles, quality of life and quality of care: Vol. 2. The elderly of New York City: A demographic and economic profile.* New York: The New York Center for Policy on Aging of the New York Community Trust.

Carlson, B. E. (1992). Questioning the party line on family violence. *Affilia, 7*(7), 94-110.

Chen, P. N., Bell, S., Dolinsky, D., Doyle, J., & Dunn, M. (1981). Elder abuse in domestic settings. *Journal of Gerontological Social Work, 4,* 3-17.

Crystal, S. (1987). Elder abuse: The latest crisis. *Public Interest, 88,* 56-66.

Fattah, E. A., & Sacco, V. F. (1989). *Crime and victimization of the elderly.* New

York: Springer-Verlag.

Faulkner, L. (1982). Mandating the reporting of suspected cases of elder abuse: An inappropriate, ineffective and ageist response to the abuse of older adults. *Family Law Quarterly, 16*(1), 69-91.

Fredrikson, K. (1989). Adult protective services: Changes with the introduction of mandatory reporting. *Journal of Elder Abuse and Neglect, 1*(2), 59-70.

Fulmer, T., & O'Malley, T. (1987). *Inadequate care of the elderly: A health care perspective on abuse and neglect.* New York: Springer.

Gelles, R. J. (1987). *Family violence.* Newbury Park, CA: Sage.

Gilford, D. (Ed.). (1988). *The aging population in the twenty-first century: Statistics for health policy.* Washington, DC: National Academy Press.

Goleman, D. (1991, November 21). Do arrests increase the rates of repeated domestic violence? *The New York Times,* sec. C., p. 8.

Griffin, L. W., & Williams, O. J. (1992). Abuse among African-American elderly. *Journal of Family Violence, 7*(1), 19-35.

Hinkle, D, Wiersma, W., & Jurs, S. (1988). *Applied statistics for the behavioral sciences.* Boston: Houghton Mifflin Company.

Hudson, M. (1989). An analysis of the concepts of elder mistreatment, abuse and neglect. *Journal of Elder Abuse and Neglect, 1,* 5-25.

Hudson, M., & Johnson, T. (1986). Elder abuse and neglect: A review of the literature. In C. Eisdorfer (Ed.), *Annual Review of Gerontology and Geriatrics* (Vol. 6, pp. 18-134). New York: Springer.

Ivanoff, A., Smyth, N., & Finnegan, D. (1993). Social work behind bars: Preparation for field work in correctional institutions. *Journal of Teaching in Social Work, 7*(1), 137-149.

Johnson, T. (1986). Critical issues in the definition of elder mistreatment. In K. Pillemer & R. Wolf (Eds.), *Elder abuse: Conflict in the Family* (pp. 167-196). Dover, MA: Auburn House.

Johnson, T. (1991). *Elder mistreatment: Deciding who is at risk.* New York: Greenwood Press.

Kim, R. (1993, May 9). Asians' fear, loathing. *Newsday,* p. 42.

Kachigan, S. (1986). *Statistical analysis: An interdisciplinary introduction to univariate and multivariate methods.* New York: Radius Press.

Lau, E., & Kosberg, J. (1979, September-October). Abuse of the elderly by informal care providers. *Aging,* pp. 10-15.

Legal Aid Society. (1993, November 14). *New York Times.* Longres, J. (1992). Race and type of maltreatment in an elder abuse system. *Journal of Elder Abuse and Neglect, 4*(3), 61-83.

Mancuso, P. J., Jr. (1989). Domestic violence and the police: Theory, policy and practice. In L. J. Dickstein & C. C. Nadelson (Eds.), *Family violence: Emerging issues of a national crisis* (pp. 127-141). Washington, DC: American Psychiatric Press.

McElroy, J. E., Cosgrove, C. A., & Sadd, S. (1993). *Community policing: The CPOP in New York.* Newbury Park, CA: Sage.

McQuillan, A. (1986, 25 April). Police briefed on abuse of elderly. *The Staten Island Advance*, p. c4.

Moon, A., & Williams, O. (1993). Perceptions of elder abuse and help-seeking patterns among African-American, Caucasian, and Korean-American elderly women. *The Gerontologist, 33*, 386-394.

National Aging Resource Center for Elder Abuse (NARCEA). (1991). *Elder abuse and neglect: A national research agenda.* Washington, DC: Author.

New York City Department for the Aged. (1993). *Borough and community district profiles of older New Yorkers.* New York: DFTA.

Passeth, P., & Bengston, V. (1988). Sociological theories of aging: Current perspectives and future directions. In J. Birren & V. Bengston (Eds.). *Emergent theories of aging* (pp. 333-355). New York: Springer.

Pillemer, K., & Finkelhor, D. (1988). The prevalence of elder abuse: A random sample survey. *The Gerontologist, 28*(1), 51-57.

Pillemer, K., & Finkelhor, D. (1989). Causes of elder abuse: Caregiver versus problem relatives. *American Orthopsychiatric Association, 59*, 179-187.

Pillemer, K., & Suitor, J. (1988). Elder abuse. In V. P. Van Hasselt, R. L. Morrison, A. S. Bellack, & M. Herson (Eds.), *Handbook of family violence* (pp. 247-270). New York: Plenam Press.

Plotkin, M. (1988). *A time for dignity: Police and domestic abuse of the elderly.* Washington, DC: PERF and AARP.

Quinn, M. J., & Tomita, S. (1997). *Elder abuse and neglect: Causes, diagnosis and intervention strategies*, Second Edition. New York: Springer Publishing Company.

Quinn, M. J., & Tomita, S. (1986). *Elder abuse and neglect: Causes, diagnosis and intervention strategies.* New York: Springer Publishing Company.

Ryan, J. (1990, March). Presentation at conference, New York City Coalition on Elder Abuse.

Saltzman, L., Mercy, J. A., Rosenberg, M. L., Elsea, W. R., Napper, G., Sikes, R. K., & Waxweiler, R. J. (1990). Magnitude and patterns of family and intimate assault in Atlanta, Georgia, 1984. *Violence and Victims, 5*(1), 3-17.

Sengstock, M., & Liang, J. (1982). *Identifying and characterizing elder abuse.*

Detroit, MI: Wayne State University, Institute of Gerontology.

Sherman, L., & Cohn, E. (1990). The effect of research on legal policy in the Minneapolis domestic violence experiment. In D. Beshanov (Ed.), *Family violence and public policy issues* (pp. 205-227). Washington, DC: American Enterprise Institute Press.

Steinmetz, S. (1978). *Duty bound: Elder abuse and family care.* Newbury Park, CA: Sage Press.

Steinmetz, S. (1981, January-February). Elder abuse. *Aging,* pp. 6-10.

Stoller, E. P., Forster, L. E., & Duniho, T. S. (1992). Systems of parent care within sibling networks. *Research on Aging, 14*(1), 28-49.

SYSTAT. (1992). *CART: Tree structured nonparametric data analysis: A SYSTAT companion product.* Evanston, IL: Author.

U.S. Department of Justice. (1981). *Measuring crime* (Special Report). Washington, DC: U.S. Government Printing Office.

U.S. Department of Justice. (1984). *Family violence* (Special Report). Washington, DC: U.S. Government Printing Office.

U.S. House of Representatives, Select Committee on Aging. (1990). *Elder abuse: Decade of shame and inaction.* Washington, DC: U.S. Government Printing Office.

U.S. House of Representatives, Committee on Ways and Means. (1993). *Overview of entitlement programs: Green book.* Washington, DC: U.S. Government Printing Office.

Vinton, L. W. (1988). *Correlates of elder abuse.* Unpublished doctoral dissertation, University of Wisconsin, Madison, WI.

Wolf, R. (1988). Elder abuse: Ten years later. *The Journal of the American Geriatrics Society, 36,* 758-762.

Wolf, R. (1990). Perpetrators of elder abuse. In R. Ammerman & M. Hersen (Eds.), *Treatment of Family Violence: A Sourcebook* (pp. 310-327). New York: J. Wiley & Sons.

Wolf, R. (1992). Victimization of the elderly: Elder abuse and neglect. *Reviews in Clinical Gerontology, 2,* 269-276.

Wolf, R., & McCarthy, E. R. (1991). Elder abuse. In R. T. Ammerman & M. Hersen (Eds.), *Case studies in family violence* (pp. 357-377). New York: Plenum Press.

Wolf, R., & Pillemer, K. (1984). *Working with abused elderly: Assessment, advocacy and intervention.* Wooster, MA: University Center on Aging, University of Massachusetts Medical Center.

Wolf, R., Strugnell, C., & Godkin, M. (1982). *Preliminary findings from three model projects on elder abuse.* Worchester, MA: University of Massachusetts Medical Center, Center on Aging, Worchester.

Wolf, R., Godkin, M., & Pillemer, K. (1984). *Elder abuse and neglect: Final report from the three model projects on elder abuse.* Wooster, MA: University of Massachusetts Center on Aging.

Yin, P. (1985). *Victimization and the Aged.* Springfield, IL: Thomas C. Charles.

Index